THE LANGUAGE OF GLOBAL SUCCESS

The Language of Global Success

How a Common Tongue Transforms Multinational Organizations

Tsedal Neeley

PRINCETON UNIVERSITY PRESS

PRINCETON AND OXFORD

Published by Princeton University Press,
41 William Street, Princeton, New Jersey 08540

In the United Kingdom: Princeton University Press,
6 Oxford Street, Woodstock, Oxfordshire OX20 1TR

press.princeton.edu

ISBN 978-0-691-17537-9

Library of Congress Control Number 2017944328

British Library Cataloging-in-Publication Data is available

This book has been composed in Adobe Text and Gotham

Printed on acid-free paper. ∞

Printed in the United States of America

10 9 8 7 6 5 4 3 2 1

To my parents, my first inspiring global teachers

CONTENTS

THE LANGUAGE OF GLOBAL SUCCESS

Introduction

"If as one people speaking the same language they have begun to do this, then nothing they plan to do will be impossible for them. Come, let us go down and confuse their language so they will not understand each other." So the Lord scattered them from there over all the earth, and they stopped building the city.

—THE TOWER OF BABEL (GENESIS 11:1–9)

They saw what seemed to be tongues of fire that separated and came to rest on each of them. . . . A crowd came together in bewilderment, because each one heard their own language being spoken. Utterly amazed, they asked: "Aren't all these who are speaking Galileans? Then how is it that each of us hears them in our native language?"

—THE HOLY SPIRIT COMES AT PENTECOST (ACTS 2:1–11)

Two well-known stories from the ancients showcase the fundamental role that language plays in human interaction and demonstrate its power to be a prelude to chaos or a herald of new understanding. The story of the tower of Babel testifies to the inevitable scattering that follows linguistic confusion. When communication breaks down, no one can move forward; they are unable to understand or be understood. Big plans come to nothing. In contrast, the story of the

Pentecost demonstrates how, despite differences in "native language," it is possible for each person in the crowd to understand perfectly what is being said. Although they originate in different cultures and locations, the people are no longer separated from one another; they are joined in clarity.

Today, language holds a similar weight in global organizations as it did for the confused people in the story of Babel and the amazed onlookers in the story of the Pentecost. There is urgency for global employees to communicate effectively so that all can engage and participate in the work required, and indeed, global organizations are at the frontier of changes in language use. For over three decades, American and British political, economic, and technological power on the world's stage has propelled English as the *lingua franca* (common language) of international business. Approximately 52 percent of multinationals today use English for some capacity of cross-border work. Yet despite the clearly established link between language and societal macro-forces, there is a surprising absence of research into how shifts in language and culture play out longitudinally at the organizational level. Adopting a lingua franca, which by definition is foreign to a portion of the employees, is not only a matter of mastering vocabulary lists and grammatical tenses. Nor is it simply a matter of having to learn the particular culture that any given language is said to embody; learning French certainly doesn't bestow knowledge of fine cheeses, nor does learning Farsi carry a proclivity for knotting intricate carpets.

I have studied the lingua franca phenomenon in global organizations for nearly fifteen years. The seed of my interest was first planted when I was part of a study at Stanford University examining the cross-cultural experience of globally dispersed teams at a German high-tech company. As many as 70 percent of employees we interviewed in Germany, India, and the United States attributed collaboration hardships of one sort or another to language. One of my first interviewees teared up when describing an ongoing sense of ostracism as a result of other team members' habitual switch to a foreign language. Others described difficulty speaking the dominant language as the source of isolation in their teams and their organizations. Many saw language differences as the most divisive aspect of their global teamwork.

As soon as I left those interviews, I turned to the literature to make sense of what I had heard. I was surprised to find very little existing research that could explain the emotionally charged experiences that employees had recounted, and even more surprised that such a knowledge gap existed about one of the most fundamental means for global workers to communicate. Since that first study, I have been motivated to go as deep and wide as I could to systematically study and write about language and the role it plays in global work.

The story of how language can affect employees and organizations in the course of a lingua franca adoption, and consequently, how our previously held notions of language and culture become upended, especially in one e-commerce high-tech giant—Rakuten—is the subject of this book. Rakuten is a leader in Japan's e-commerce space, and its CEO is regarded as a maverick in business and cultural change, but its challenges with language and cultural diversity are germane to many global organizations.

Founded in June 1997 in Japan as an e-mall service, Rakuten Ichiba was part of the mid-1990s Internet growth that ushered in an era in which the buying and selling of products and services moved online in what has become the e-commerce industry. Although in the past two decades traditional brick-and-mortar retail businesses have increasingly adopted online shopping capabilities or participated in third-party online marketplaces, Rakuten has been strictly an e-commerce business from its founding. Approximately 75 percent of growth in retail sales since 2000 can be attributed to e-commerce.[1] In Japan and elsewhere, this surge was driven in large part by the growth in Internet accessibility, with 46 percent of global households having access to the Internet and 43 percent of people globally using the Internet in 2015.[2] Consumers increasingly look globally for e-commerce purchases of products otherwise unobtainable in their domestic market and because they are motivated by lower prices, greater selection, higher quality of products, and assurance against product counterfeiting.[3]

Rakuten's platform allowed retailers, product manufacturers, and other service providers to build online storefronts, operating within a B2B2C (Business to Business to Consumer) model. Major consumer electronics retailers sold Sony, NEC, Nintendo, Panasonic, or Hitachi-branded items on Rakuten's platform. In return, Rakuten generated revenues from its merchants (retailers) through fixed monthly fees, sales of advertising and other services, and a percentage of gross merchandise sales. As the intermediary between sellers and buyers, Rakuten did not handle inventory for the vast majority of its business (books and media were the only exceptions). Rakuten later expanded into other Internet services, including cashback sites, travel-booking sites, and digital content, such as e-books and video streaming, as well as financial services, including Internet banking, online securities trading, a Rakuten-issued credit card, and life insurance.[4] Rakuten also pursued online mobile messaging and communication, management of its professional baseball team, the Tohoku Rakuten Golden Eagles, and other niche businesses. Similar to Amazon.com, which also pioneered e-commerce before diversifying its businesses into online payments, e-readers, digital content, and cloud infrastructure services, Rakuten would eventually host business services in the global marketplace.[5]

In March 2010 the CEO of Rakuten, Hiroshi Mikitani, mandated a company-wide English language initiative, effective immediately. I learned about Englishnization at Rakuten several months later and began to interview employees and conduct what would become a five-year, in-depth, longitudinal study of Rakuten's English language strategy. Throughout the study, Mikitani granted me total access to his company, inviting me to go anywhere in the world to talk to any of his employees and without imposing a single condition. I talked with people as many times as I deemed necessary to develop a rich understanding of lingua franca and cultural phenomena as they unfolded in real time. I employed a hybrid approach to collect qualitative, quantitative, and archival data. The qualitative data comprised 650 interviews across eight country sites—Brazil, France, Germany, Indonesia, Japan (headquarters), Taiwan, Thailand, and the United States—that were conducted in five languages. The quantitative data were collected at two points in time, totaling 3,056 surveys. I also collected over 20,000 pages of archival documents. The data I collected eventually informed the findings that I present as Phase One and Phase Two, capturing two key stages of the lingua franca adoption processes. Further details about my research methods can be found in appendices A and B, where I delineate how I analyzed the quantitative data.

As I reviewed and analyzed the data, three distinct social groups emerged and led me to conceive of workers in the global organization as expatriates in their own countries. Expatriates (often shortened to "expats") are people temporarily or permanently residing as immigrants in a country other than that of their citizenship. I have repurposed the word "expat" to mean people who are temporarily or permanently detached from their mother tongue or home culture while still operating in their own country. The change to a lingua franca is the catalyst for all employees to become an expat of one sort or another in their daily organizational work while still living in their native country. The expat perspective that I conceptualize rests on the assumption that everyone is at least slightly uncomfortable detaching from a native language or culture.

This book lies at the intersection of language, national culture, and organizational culture, and before we go any further, let me say a little more about definitions. Here, "language" means the lingua franca. "Culture" refers to a national culture—for example, Japanese, American, German, Thai, or others. My definition of "organizational culture" is one articulated by O'Reilly and Chatman as "a system of shared values (that define what is important) and norms that define appropriate attitudes and behaviors for organizational members (how to feel and behave)."[6]

Theoretical and empirical focus on language and globalization continues to dramatically lag the realities that employees face on the ground, as will become apparent in this book. Understanding the evolution of a language mandate over time and across groups enables us to develop insights into how people who work in global organizations learn to communicate and negotiate linguistic and cultural differences. Language is everywhere. It flows across and touches the entire spectrum of global organizational processes: values, norms, attitudes, customer service work, product design, marketing, hiring, evaluating, and promoting employees, internal reporting, post-merger integration, innovation, process improvements, teaming, and much more. A language change affects these processes and practices simultaneously.

In addition, my study of the lingua franca mandate and employees' experience at Rakuten demonstrates that a foreign language can be appropriated and used as a conduit to spread a native culture. In looking closely at how English lingua franca is currently used in a global workplace, I discovered what can happen when a language and culture are productively *de*coupled. I unpack the ways in which the English language transported Japanese national cultural traditions and beliefs throughout the globalizing organization at Rakuten. I draw attention to the ramifications of the decoupling of language and culture throughout the book. As I studied these ramifications over a five-year period, I found that each of the three social groups that emerged at Rakuten grappled with and eventually found a way to integrate the changes—linguistic, cultural, or both—that were a consequence of the firm-wide lingua franca adoption.

The first group comprised employees who lived in their home country, Japan, yet had to give up their mother tongue when they entered their place of employment or signed into a conference call. Their organization demanded that they shed the ease of their native language, making their daily work experience fraught with language challenges. Conceptually, one might think it is comparable to immigrants' transformative experience of having to learn and adopt a foreign language when moving to a foreign country; however, the twist, one that fundamentally alters how we understand what it means to adopt a new language, is that they had to do so while remaining in their home country. I call this group *linguistic expats* precisely because they became language expatriates in their own country.

The second group comprised native English-speaking employees who lived and worked in Rakuten's U.S. subsidiaries. Initially, the native English-speaking employees were euphoric when the CEO stipulated the English lingua franca mandate. The vast majority of the native English-speaking employees initially felt privileged; they believed that they were the beneficiaries of the change, having increased capacity to contribute to the organization and anticipating myriad new opportunities for career advancement. This group did in fact become beneficiaries of improved communication, but what eventually happened, once the Japanese employees became more proficient in English, overturned their—and my—assumptions. Contrary to expectation, the company-wide mandate to adopt the English language became a gateway for the spread of Rakuten's organizational culture—one built on the Japanese national identity—into the U.S. subsidiaries.

The Americans' sense of good fortune—that they happened to be native English speakers operating in their home country—fell away with the onslaught of foreign organizational and cultural values into their daily work practices and processes. As this group struggled to adjust to such new practices as being monitored by supervisors to ensure they were wearing the prescribed Rakuten badge, correctly pinned, at all times, they became *cultural expats*—forced to detach from their native cultural norms and adopt organizational cultural practices that rubbed against their American grain. The fundamental twist for this group was that the shift to their native language ironically opened the door to cultural changes in organizational practices more reflective of Japanese national culture than of their own native culture, within which they were working.

The third group also surprised me. It was composed of employees who were neither native English speakers nor members of the Japanese-headquartered native group. Rather, they worked in Rakuten's non-native English-speaking foreign offices: Brazil, France, Germany, Indonesia, Taiwan, and Thailand. One might expect that those who had to shed their foundational languages *and* cultures, who were *linguistic-cultural* (or *dual*) *expats* in their home country, would have experienced a double jeopardy. This group had the easier linguistic adjustment to English and the easier cultural adjustment to the Japanese ways ushered in by the lingua franca mandate, although they too had to master steep learning curves to gain higher language proficiency and engage in new culturally unfamiliar work practices.

Once the dual expats overcame the frustrations of communicating and coordinating work across borders, they were surprisingly open and receptive to languages and cultural practices that were foreign to their locale, nationality, or identity. These attitudes are what will make dual expats, in my estimation, the employee group most likely to be effective for global organizations of the twenty-first century.

There is a fourth category, bilingual employees, that deserves brief mention. Fluent in Japanese and English, they were playing a necessary intermediary role in the organization pre-mandate. This small group, who held positions in every division (e.g., engineering, human resources), also served as translators between colleagues. However, after the lingua franca mandate took hold and people's language fluency evolved, the demand for these bilinguals lessened and then became nearly nonexistent because they were no longer unique. I do not focus on this group because they represent a very small subset of the employee population, and consequently I do not have sufficient data to capture as robust a story as I was able to develop for the other three groups, though I touch on them in chapter 6.

Adopting an expat frame allows me to look closely at how a workforce meets the challenges of belonging to a global organization. My hope is that after reading this book, scholars and practitioners will be sensitive to the fact that each of the three social groups—linguistic expats, cultural expats, and dual expats—has new roles and responsibilities to themselves and to the organization. A lingua franca mandate leaves no organizational process or practice untouched. In ways tangible and intangible, superficial and profound, the organization itself is changed.

While some aspects of my analysis are unique to Rakuten—its e-commerce industry, the Japanese corporate and national culture in which it is embedded, its charismatic CEO, and the comprehensive approach he took to rolling out the lingua franca mandate—there are lessons to be learned for many global companies as they will likely confront similar language and culture challenges. The reality is that both kinds of challenges are already occurring within firms that operate across national boundaries. The experiences of the three social groups I identify provide theoretical and empirical purchase in our understanding of workers in global organizations. Importantly, the expat perspective allows us to see the extent to which some people will feel linguistically estranged, others will feel culturally estranged, and some will experience distances on both ends depending on whether they are native or non-native members.

There are two organizational scenarios that are likely to give rise to these three social groups. The first scenario is global organizations with an English lingua franca that are headquartered in an English-speaking country—for example, the United States, the United Kingdom, or Australia—and thus do not have linguistic expats but do have cultural expats and dual expats in their workforce. The second scenario consists of the reverse; in organizations that adopt an English lingua franca and are headquartered in a country where the native language is *not* English—for example, Brazil, Germany, or China—linguistic expats, cultural expats, and linguistic-cultural expats are likely to exist. In organizations where English is both the native language and the lingua franca, people may still categorize as cultural expats if there is a mismatch between the culture of the headquarters and that of the subsidiary. For example, an Australian employee who is part of a U.S.-based organization would be required to adhere to American values and cultural norms. Australians become cultural expats because they share a common native language with their U.S. employer (English), while still having to adapt to different cultural norms (American). On the other hand, Malaysian employees of that same company who work in Malaysia would hold the position of dual expats when they must adopt a non-native language (English) and operate within a non-native organization (U.S.) and national culture (American).

If we look at the alternative scenario, an organization situated in a country where the native language is not English, then all three categories of employees (linguistic expats, cultural expats, and dual expats) would likely exist, similar to the situation at Rakuten. For example, if a company is headquartered in Germany and adopts the English lingua franca (e.g., SAP or Siemens), employees who work in Germany would fall into the linguistic expat category. Employees who are native English speakers would be cultural expats, while those who are non-native English speakers and non-Germans would fall into the linguistic expat categories.

In the end, each social group has distinct challenges and rewards. Regardless of where each social group begins, the book takes the reader through the separate journey each group followed to become expats in their own countries. With the exception of the CEO and select executives who have spoken publicly about the language strategy, I refer to interviewees by pseudonyms to protect their identities.

Chapter 1 sets the stage with the dramatic announcement by Hiroshi Mikitani, CEO of Rakuten, informing his 10,000 employees, of which over 7,100 are Japanese nationals, that from that day forward they must speak English in the workplace. In two years, they will be required to clear a proficiency test or risk demotion. In this first chapter we meet three employees who represent the categories that make up the core of the book: Kenji, a Japanese engineer gripped by shock and fear that his years of hard work with the company will count for naught, who then receives the technical and emotional support to practice new English language skills; Robert, a native English-speaking marketing manager from the United States, thrilled that the company is switching to his native language and who anticipates an easy career advance only to have his sense of privilege curtailed by new, daily work requirements, followed by a trip to Japan where his cultural blinders begin to loosen; and a German IT technician, Inga, pleased by the announcement, who hopes it will streamline her work process—and learns that it does once she climbs the steep and often frustrating learning curve. To contextualize this chapter, I weave in trends, theories, and empirical evidence that deepen our understanding of the development and effects of English as a lingua franca in global organizations more broadly.

Chapter 2 follows Mikitani's thinking and leadership development with regard to the Englishnization mandate. Initially, Mikitani believed the English language mandate would succeed if employees were independent and entrepreneurial, taking full responsibility—financially and otherwise—for learning English. However, after nearly a year and a half, upon discovering that progress was dismal, he led a major shift. I introduce and discuss Mikitani's promotion of the mandate during the second phase of "English only"—learning English while retaining one's native culture. I assess how Mikitani's leadership influenced employee attitudes and English language proficiency scores.

Chapters 3, 4, and 5 follow the three employees introduced in chapter 1 and draw from the experiences of others similarly positioned in the organization to trace, through an expat perspective, how each group develops and changes over time. Importantly, the expat perspective provides new insights about the interplay between language and culture. What does it mean for employees to detach from their original language or culture, and for some, both? Chapter 3 focuses on the Japanese linguistic expats and their linguistic shock, which initially presents a barrier to learning a foreign language. The results of the seemingly insurmountable challenge at the mandate's announcement—base English language proficiency for the Japanese domestic workforce—are provided and discussed in chapter 3. Chapter 4, which focuses on the native English-speaking cultural expats, takes up the corresponding culture shock they undergo as a result of inundation from a foreign (Japanese) culture, presenting a barrier to cross-cultural communication. Chapter 5, about the linguistic-cultural expats, describes how this group's lack of either linguistic or cultural shock eventually presents the lowest barrier to living in and learning a foreign culture. This process, although challenging for many individuals in the first two groups, emerged as freeing for the dual expat employees and allowed them entry to more adaptive attitudes and behaviors.

Chapter 6 documents the largely beneficial results of the lingua franca mandate on Rakuten over a period of five years, including the rise in international acquisitions, accelerated post-integration activities, centralized technical platforms, and knowledge sharing. An expanded and global talent pool changed hiring patterns within the Tokyo headquarters and worldwide, particularly in the engineering ranks. While many advances were made in the advent of the English language mandate, this chapter also highlights enduring challenges.

In addition, chapter 6 shows examples of Rakuten's influence beyond the confines of the organization. When I first met Hiroshi

Mikitani, he told me that he was passionate about empowering and renewing Japanese society and that he viewed Rakuten as an important conduit for societal-level changes. The English language mandate was chief among the changes that his company could effect nationally, particularly because Mikitani's globalization ambitions for his company were deeply intertwined with his ambitions for Japan. The prime minister of Japan tapped Mikitani to join a newly formed advisory body, the Industrial Competitiveness Council, to aid in developing a globalization agenda. A national language strategy was rooted in the actions that the council adopted. These activities demonstrate the role that companies can have in shaping societal growth and character.

Chapter 7 considers how the insights from this research and other in-depth work that I have conducted can serve as a guide for practitioners at three levels in the organization—top leaders, managers, and employees—who are seeking to better navigate shifts as they adopt practices for their organizations' lingua franca and cultural transitions. I detail the factors that top leaders need to consider when assessing the appropriateness of a lingua franca and corresponding implementation tactics. Without a broader understanding of how language changes affect their workforce, and what is needed for implementation, many organizations will falter in their lingua franca mandates. I also highlight how managers can practically support and accurately evaluate employees who are operating in a cross-lingua environment. Finally, the chapter provides communication strategies for employees in their everyday interactions globally.

Language can affect every aspect of global organizational life. If leaders can integrate language changes effectively, they will open untold opportunities to unleash previously untapped talent in their workforce and increase their company's ability to maximize what is too often an unfulfilled promise of globalization. A lingua franca is the closest we have to the "tongues of fire" that allow people to hear and comprehend any language as if it were their own. Only by learning to communicate—with words and culture—can we go forward, into the future world and work of global business.

1

The Lingua Franca Mandate

"ENGLISHNIZATION"

On Monday, March 1, 2010, Hiroshi Mikitani stepped to the podium at the Tokyo headquarters of his company, Rakuten. At forty-four, Mikitani was the billionaire celebrity CEO of Japan's largest online retailer and was renowned for making daring business decisions, made all the more controversial in Japan, where conformity and tradition are esteemed. Fourteen years earlier, he had left an enviable career at the Industrial Bank of Japan to launch Rakuten with a small founding team. By 2010, his company was a household name and Internet destination of choice for the majority of Japanese online shoppers. Mikitani was often dubbed the Bill Gates and Jeff Bezos of Japan for his prescience in seeing the changes technology would bring to commerce and for the acumen he had demonstrated in Rakuten's meteoric rise.

Mikitani adjusted the microphone. These weekly company-wide meetings, called Asakai, were attended by over seven thousand Japanese employees—crowded into an enormous auditorium, often weaving around the corner and into an overflow room—and by a loyal contingent of Rakuten's three thousand overseas employees who watched via video. Most of the managers watching remotely understood little Japanese, but they liked watching their charismatic CEO in action. Later, they would receive translated summaries of his speech.

On this particular day, Mikitani had an announcement that departed from the usual format. He spoke from the podium in English. "For the first time in the entire history of Rakuten," he said, "we held today's executive meeting in English. Many executives struggled quite a bit, but we managed to get through the entire agenda." As the audience strained to listen he announced that "our goal is to catch up with the global market. To step up to this challenge we must try to change our language gradually from Japanese to English. This is going to be a long-term effort for us. Starting this month, my own speech will simply be in English." Mikitani went on to explain why he believed it was critical for Rakuten in particular and the country of Japan in general to acquire proficiency in English.

Language, he insisted, was the bottleneck that precluded the organization from leveraging valuable business knowledge that had accrued within the Japanese headquarters and existing subsidiaries. A common language was the only way to extend knowledge sharing across the organization's existing global operations, as well as those that would be newly and rapidly established in order to efficiently achieve business results. He reminded his employees that Rakuten aspired to deploy operations in twenty-seven countries and raise the overseas portion of their revenue to 70 percent within ten years. An important market for the e-commerce global growth strategy was the U.S. market, in line with companies like Amazon and eBay, where English proficiency would clearly be necessary. The Tokyo office was then steadily hiring engineers from India and China who spoke English, but not Japanese. Mikitani said what was perhaps most difficult for his workforce to hear: he wanted to continue expanding his talent pool and sought to hire non-Japanese workers for the Tokyo office as well as elsewhere in the company.

Finally, there was the shrinking Japanese GDP. Mikitani told his audience: "By 2050, Japanese GDP as a portion of global GDP will shrink from 12 percent in 2006 to 3 percent." Fast and direct communication—without the cumbersome time delays that translation incurred—was the only way to integrate his business across multiple nations and insert his company effectively in non-Japanese markets. He reminded his workforce that "our goal is not becoming number one in Japan but becoming the number one Internet services company in the world. As we consider the future potential growth of the Japanese market and our company, global implementation is not a nice-to-have but a must-do." And he promised that changing the language employees spoke would affect more than just communication. It would revolutionize how Rakuten workers saw themselves and interacted with the rest of the world.

Mikitani saved the bombshell of his speech for last. By April 1, 2012, two years from the first all-English meeting, Rakuten employees would be required to score above 650 on the 990-point Test of English for International Communication (TOEIC)[1] or face the consequences. If his audience did not understand the precise wording they would soon feel its impact. Mikitani promised: "We will demote people who really do not try hard. We will monitor their progress and their test scores, and I will get reports from all the managers about employee progress." Soon after, he instructed division heads to provide monthly reports on the average TOEIC scores of their employees relative to the desired target.

By the next morning, Japanese language cafeteria menus were replaced with their English equivalents. English replaced Japanese floor directories in Rakuten elevators. Even the corporate executives were stunned. Mikitani had not consulted with them before announcing his decision because he had assumed they would resist the idea of a full-on English conversion. Instead, by announcing the mandate directly to the entire company, he made the policy immediate and irreversible. In Mikitani's mind, the future of Rakuten and Japan depended on what he called "Englishnization" and was too crucial to postpone. He had invented the term to embody what he called an unprecedented, radical idea for a Japanese company.[2] One of Rakuten's most critical principles, "Speed!! Speed!! Speed!!" was in action. Englishnization had begun full force.

Global Organizations and Language

The style in which Rakuten mandated a common language may have been unusual, but the adoption of English was in step with the practice of global organizations. Multinationals adopt a lingua franca[3] for at least four reasons. First, the pressure to grow globally, as well as the mergers and acquisitions that often cross national and linguistic boundaries, drive organizations to find a common way to communicate.[4] Second, translators and interpreters for everyday work relationships tend to be inadequate.[5] Meetings between individuals who speak different languages that rely on translators can become cumbersome and unnecessarily lengthy; likewise, translated documents often lose nuance and slow down transactions. Third, the absence of a lingua franca makes it challenging for linguistically diverse, and usually geographically dispersed, employees to share knowledge and collaborate. It has been long established that global team members who do not share the same language struggle to convey tacit knowledge that will advance their organization's goals.[6] Finally, when subsidiaries are unable to communicate with their headquarters in the same language, the organization can find it difficult and inefficient to communicate a shared mission and values.[7]

On the other hand, research demonstrates that a lingua franca not only enables a company to have better external and internal communication but also can promote a sense of belonging for employees located worldwide[8] and serve as a reminder of the organization's global vision.[9] Over the last three decades, English has overwhelmingly become the most commonly adopted lingua franca. According to linguist David Crystal, one in four people in the world now speak a useful level of English and there are over one billion fluent speakers. English's flexible grammar and lack of masculine and feminine forms make it relatively easy to learn. Its centuries-long habit of integrating vocabulary from other countries—"bonsai," "kamikaze," "tycoon," and "sushi," to cite a few Japanese contributions—lends it a familiarity to learners.[10]

However, history has also shown that a language becomes global not because of intrinsic properties but because of the military, economic, and political dominance of its native speakers.[11] Just as Greek, Latin, and Arabic were once the common languages of international communication at the height of their respective empires, English as a lingua franca is due in large part to the long history of colonial Britain and the superpower position of the United States.[12] The consensus is clear: not only has English become the common language spoken around the globe, but it is the fastest-spreading lingua franca in human history.[13] Linguist John McWhorter points out, "English is dominant in a way that no language has ever been before."[14] As will be further detailed in chapter 5, scholars at MIT have found English to be the number one written language worldwide, signaling its overriding influence in communication.[15]

Global companies from nearly all the major industries—Audi, Atos, Deutsche Bank, IBM, Lufthansa, Microsoft, Nokia, Nestlé, Samsung, SAP, Uber, and the list goes on—are already requiring employees to use English. By mandating English, Rakuten was prepared to join the approximately 52 percent of multinational companies that had adopted a language different from that of their originating country in order to better meet global expansion and business needs.[16]

Initial Employee Responses

Rakuten employees were astonished by Hiroshi Mikitani's radical announcement of the Englishnization mandate. This abrupt change that would soon affect all aspects of their work life also provoked a bevy of emotions.

Kenji (36), an engineer, could not believe what he had just heard. Kenji had seen Rakuten grow by leaps and bounds in the previous eight years. He had always admired Hiroshi Mikitani, and it was in these company-wide Asakai meetings that he grew accustomed to hearing the CEO's ambitious goals for the company and its workforce. Today's announcement was different and seemed nearly impossible to believe. Did he just hear Mikitani say that the official language of Rakuten was going to be English? Would his salary really be linked to his English ability?

Kenji had never traveled outside his island nation of Japan. Like nearly everyone in Japan, he had studied English for six years during middle and high school, but he had graduated with a minimal ability to understand English—and even this smattering of comprehension had long been forgotten. Suddenly thrust into a situation where he would be forced to learn a new language later in life or face demotion, Kenji felt like he was at a colossal disadvantage. He felt that his eight years of diligent, hard work in service to Rakuten should speak for itself, yet now—no matter how hard he worked—it wouldn't amount to anything without English. As a "salaryman" who expected job security in exchange for diligence and loyalty, Kenji was gripped by total shock and fear.

Robert (29), a marketing manager, was viewing the meeting remotely from New York. Watching the meeting live was highly unusual for him because of the significant time difference and language barrier. In the past, he had made it a priority to start his week by reading the translated transcripts of the meeting, which disseminated throughout the company. Robert grew excited as he heard Mikitani speaking in English. Even more surprising was Mikitani's declaration that Rakuten's Japanese workforce would shift to English for all internal communication. He was thrilled at the announcement, and also relieved that Mikitani had picked his native language. Having worked for the company for only two years, he instantly imagined the many ways the decision could positively impact his daily work and potentially even his career trajectory.

When Robert started working for Rakuten, his interactions with his Japanese counterparts were few and far between. Translators were necessary in nearly every exchange with Japan, whether it was an e-mail, phone call, videoconference, or in-person visit from headquarters staff. Even these limited interactions bred frustrations because a brief meeting could easily run twice as long as a typical U.S. meeting. Translators were also not immune from misunderstandings. Robert imagined how these issues would change for the better if lines of communication were direct. Gone would be the struggle to discern information from e-mails, PowerPoint slides, or other documents written in Japanese to even determine if they were relevant to his job. As a native English speaker, he anticipated that there would be great things around the corner for him. Experiences he previously could only dream of could now become a reality.

Inga (30) worked in the information technology department in Germany. The scope of her daily work included development of the e-commerce platform and other software for internal use. As someone who was moderately fluent in English, Inga was pleased with the English language announcement. Communicating in a mix of English and her native German would be a natural extension of what was already commonplace at work. She hoped that day-to-day communication in English would help the German office gain more insights from Japan that would assist in further developing the local market.

Historically, most of the IT documentation received from headquarters had been in Japanese. A recent example was fresh in Inga's mind. Several days into developing a prototype for a technology platform, Inga hit a roadblock and could not move forward without vital information from her Japanese colleagues. It took her several days to get what she needed. She hoped that a standard language would make information readily accessible. What now took several days might someday soon take several minutes. Inga had worked in Germany for a company with an English lingua franca before joining Rakuten and believed that the shift to English was normal for a global company where people needed to communicate across countries. She hoped that English would allow her to overcome not only language barriers but also the cross-cultural differences inherent in cross-border communication.

Over the next eighteen months, as Englishnization became central to daily life at Rakuten, I found that Kenji, Robert, and Inga came to embody the three central types of experiences that employees underwent as the company's culture and business practices transformed. In chapters 3, 4, and 5, I will elaborate on these crucial categories of experiences and responses and on how employees adapted (positively and negatively) to the global, English-only work shift in the organization.

Public Responses

Employees were not the only ones who had responses to Mikitani's announcement. News organizations around the globe picked up the

Englishnization story instantly—over a hundred articles appeared in leading sources like CNN, the *Financial Times*, the *Japan Times*, and the *Wall Street Journal*. Corporate Japan reacted with both fascination and disdain. In a culture where deference takes precedence over public criticism, the magnitude of Mikitani's mandate was evidenced by Honda Motors CEO Takanobu Ito's public assertion: "It's stupid for a Japanese company to only use English in Japan when the workforce is mainly Japanese."[17]

Mikitani was unshaken. His response to criticism was consistent: "I don't react. I just ignore it. I am trying to make Rakuten a globally successful company. It's a good thing for employees—in both their professional and personal lives—because English will open up their vision to what's happening all over the world. I would like to open our eyes." Quite correctly, he surmised, "I'm sure that other companies will regret it [not switching to English]. They will follow us if we become successful." Three years later, Honda made English the official business language for global meetings,[18] and in 2015 they committed to making English their official language within the company.[19] Mikitani pointed to the decision already made by another globalizing Japanese firm, clothes retailer Uniqlo, to require English in internal meetings by 2012. He underscored his prediction for the future by adding, "I have noticed that English language schools are full these days, and not just with Rakuten employees."

Behind the Mandate: CEO Hiroshi Mikitani

Mikitani's exposure to the English language and the world beyond Japan began when he was a child. Between the ages of seven and nine, while his father was a visiting scholar at Yale University, Mikitani lived in Connecticut, garnering English language fluency and exposure to American culture. His father, an economics scholar, was among the first Japanese academics to study as a visiting professor at three major U.S. universities (Stanford, Harvard, and Yale) following World War II. His mother had spent several years in New York as a child. Back in Japan, the Mikitani family regularly hosted foreign luminaries from the world of economics; it was not uncommon to hear English spoken at the dinner table.

After completing college in Japan, Mikitani joined the Industrial Bank of Japan in 1988, attracted to its traditional mission of helping build Japan's heavy industries. While there, Mikitani worked aggressively on his English to prepare for his studies at Harvard Business School. His two-year MBA experience was transformative. For the first time in his adult life he was exposed to the idea of entrepreneurship and was intrigued by the concept that one could found a company to create value. In an environment where leadership, opportunity, and "thinking big" are emphasized, Mikitani pondered whether he could possibly start a company. A small seed had been planted. Upon graduation he returned to the Industrial Bank of Japan where he steadily moved up the corporate ladder.

Two and a half years after Mikitani returned from the United States, on a seemingly ordinary day in 1995, a devastating earthquake struck in Hanshin, Japan. This was where Mikitani had grown up and where his family still lived. He scrambled to check on the safety of his family. He was relieved to find his parents safe. However, after a desperate search, Mikitani identified the lifeless bodies of his aunt and uncle in a makeshift morgue at a local school. In deep grief, Mikitani saw that life was short. Life was fragile. Life was unpredictable. Was he really making the best of his one life? He thought of nothing else. Finally, he made the decision to resign from the Industrial Bank of Japan. He wanted to strike out on his own and act on his growing attraction toward entrepreneurship. It was now or never. Mikitani launched Rakuten's e-mall service in June 1997.

By 2010, when Mikitani introduced Englishnization, Rakuten had become the dominant player in the Japanese e-commerce domain with over ninety million customers, accounting for nearly 85 percent of the market share. Mikitani was proud to say that in Japan Rakuten was "number one in e-commerce, number one in travel, number one in banking, and number one in brokerage." He described the company as "the aggregation of all sorts of Internet services with the same brand name, the same points program . . . a unique, very dependable, and competitive business model as a group in Japan." With little room to grow in Japan, Mikitani had his sights on new international markets. Expanding globally was the only way to sustain growth. But to shift from a Japanese company to a global one required a profound change in perspective. He believed that Englishnization was key.

Japan and the Lingua Franca

Mikitani's vision for how to become a global company made him a pioneer among his Japanese cohort of business CEOs. Unlike the economies of many other industrialized countries, Japan's remained largely insular until the early 1990s. Although sluggish, its economy remained strong and the domestic market was large enough to sustain Japanese industry. However, by the early 2000s, all this was changing. Japan's economy was shrinking. Many Japanese businesses faced the reality that global expansion was necessary to remain competitive in the face of increasing corporate debt, foreign competition, and pressure on the social security system from an aging population.[20] However, conservative political leadership, workplace culture, and an educational system that supported a very nationalist view of the world colluded to make Japanese companies see global expansion as a particularly difficult task.[21]

Language presented a particular challenge for the Japanese workforce. Because of the heavy reliance on local sources of revenue, many Japanese workers never needed to communicate in a language other than Japanese. Compared to their counterparts in other countries, Japanese employees were significantly behind on foreign language adoption. In fact, in a 2008 global survey on national competitiveness, Japanese respondents were the least likely to indicate that "English education is useful and practical."[22] Similarly, a 2010 study comparing English proficiency scores across fifty-eight countries found Japan to be at the very bottom of the list.[23] Mikitani found himself on the cutting edge of the new Japanese economy, and his strategies were very much in line with analysts' predictions for what was needed to increase the competitiveness of Japanese companies.

Employees who cannot speak English are feeling inferior. At meetings, they cannot articulate their opinions. I have seen opinions accepted just because they were couched in good English, not because the content of the opinion was great.

Rakuten employees' initial feelings of lowered status in the face of Englishnization echo people's experiences in other companies undergoing similar mandates. For example, in a French tech company, native French-speaking employees who had previously viewed themselves as adequate English speakers reported feeling "stupid," "diminished," "reduced," or "devalued" after a mandate for English lingua franca went into effect. As at Rakuten, these employees felt the mandate signaled a shift in characteristics the company valued and suddenly spotlighted their inadequacies in fluency.[5]

PRODUCTIVITY, ANXIETY, AND JOB INSECURITY

The earliest attempts at Rakuten to use English provoked anxiety in employees about their ability to remain productive, which led to feelings of insecurity about holding their job. A drop in productivity was immediate at all levels and across the company. Employee statements describing productivity decrements ranged from "my productivity has greatly declined" to descriptions of newly laborious work realities.[6] For example, a team leader described a dramatic upward spike in the time it took to generate documents; a task that had taken him thirty minutes to complete in Japanese was taking him up to four hours to complete in English, in part because he had to undergo more steps to verify that the document was ready for sharing:

> We create the materials in Japanese first and then translate them into English. If some of these materials are important, we have to ask someone in our team who can speak English or native speakers to check them. It just takes much longer to prepare materials.

Another manager railed against the spike in workload for people at all ranks to adhere to the English standard:

It now takes more time to prepare for meetings (translating meeting materials, preparing a script for announcements, practicing the announcements), and handing all this over to the subordinates in the department that can do so in English is using inordinate amounts of time on the part of superiors and subordinates.

Both of these managers spoke to a difficult reality: people's responsibilities and goals remained the same, but they were required to achieve them in a language they barely knew. During the first survey, administered a little over a year after the mandate was announced, employees rated their productivity before the mandate as significantly higher than after the mandate. That sentiment was still evident six months later; Japanese respondents again rated their perceived productivity *after Englishnization* as lower than their productivity before the mandate.[7]

Understandably, the lowered productivity became a source of job insecurity. The drop in productivity did not affect the company's revenue performance, but linguistic expats' concerns about the potential adverse effects to their careers were rampant. They worried that they would be appraised for their verbal and written agility rather than their job performance. A commonly heard refrain was: "I am worried that English skill is going to be the main factor to measure my ability." A seasoned employee who had been with the organization for seven years before the lingua franca mandate explained, "I may be really good in my job, but my poor English skills may affect me." Such fears were not unfounded; Japanese employees were subject to demotions if they did not meet the English language proficiency assessment (TOEIC) threshold as stipulated. An informant explained: "Even though work performance may be good, if my TOEIC score does not reach the target, promotions will be difficult and my salary may not rise." Employees expressed resentment toward the mandate's demands with statements such as: "I don't agree with this. It will be hard for me to stay motivated" and "It is harsh to evaluate and appraise people on their English ability as a measuring stick."

In sum, Rakuten's linguistic expats worried about being misjudged professionally because of their decreased productivity and limited

English facility. Further, they feared the possible consequence of demotion (or lack of promotion) that loomed large should they fail to meet the language demands.[8] These worries and insecurities, as much as their objective proficiency (or lack thereof) in English, combined with the threat to their identities, contributed greatly to the linguistic expats' perspective—unsettled while at home.

Second Phase
ENGLISH LANGUAGE PROFICIENCY RESULTS

When the proficiency test results were finally in a little over two years post-mandate, 87 percent of employees met or exceeded the proficiency expectations.[9] The rest of the employees were granted a six-month grace period to meet their scores, resulting in an additional 3 percent of employees passing the bar. Overall, a staggering 90 percent of Japanese employees met or exceeded their required language proficiency threshold. Thereafter, those who failed to meet the requirement were subject to demotion, which translated into a downgrade in their rank and corresponding salary. If demoted, employees were given the opportunity to return to their original ranking and salary once they cleared the required proficiency threshold.

However, the language development process did not end there. Once the climate relaxed on the subject of demotions, and people were relieved of their initial intense language learning and test-prepping experiences, Mikitani raised the proficiency bar by giving everyone four years to reach a score of 800, which is the top TOEIC level. He wanted to keep the organization focused on continuous language learning and increasing proficiency. An 800 also became the mandatory requirement for all new hires; this played a role in the changing face of the company's talent, as will be discussed in chapter 6.

Five years into Rakuten's Englishnization, I was able to review the years of survey data that I had collected from the native Japanese employees. I had sets of open-ended survey questions asking employees to reflect on their experiences with the language mandate from 2011 to 2013 and then again from 2013 to 2015. After so much time had passed, I was eager to account for what the linguistic expats had learned, whether they had recovered from the language shock they'd experienced upon learning of the mandate, and if they felt more positive toward learning English than they had previously. I wanted to measure the present practice of English at Rakuten against Mikitani's 2010 visionary hopes for his workforce. What I found was in some ways encouraging regarding the feasibility of implementing a company-wide lingua franca, and in other ways, the data I collected made me realize the limitations of a single language strategy and the concomitant challenges of the whole enterprise.

The encouraging news was that by 2015, 80 percent of 183 Japanese Rakuten survey respondents asserted the importance of English. I found the same percentage to be true in the conversations I held with 50 Japanese employees during this time period. What's more, analysis of the Englishnization experience reported by linguistic expats between both the first phase and second phase evinced a striking pattern of improvements. Most of the respondents reported having achieved bounded English competencies: the ability to formally memorize reading, speaking, pronunciation, or grammar skills and to informally read or watch English language based media (for example, TED talks), to strengthen language skills.

Additional improvements included understanding the majority of exchanges during meetings and increased confidence in their abilities. As one linguistic expat put it: "I am not afraid to speak English to my coworkers, because everyone can understand English." Another reported, "Now I teach [in English] non-Japanese colleagues about IT technologies weekly." Others had progressed from an initial avoidance behavior to having a basic capacity for reading technical documentation written in English. The most advanced respondents progressed from an initial period that consisted of studying for the TOEIC test and translating Japanese materials into English to a second period of creating lengthy presentations and documents, recruiting foreign candidates, and even holding job interviews in English.

INTERMINABLE LINGUA FRANCA BOUNDED FLUENCY

The improvements, proficiency scores, and increased capacity to comprehend and communicate in the lingua franca came with much difficulty and limitations. A respondent portrayed the first phase as a struggle through pronunciation, vocabulary, and grammar books and the second phase as learning basic English and more advanced pronunciation. Another respondent shared that communicating with non-Japanese colleagues remained difficult for both phases. Yet another noted that his written English had not changed that much, but his speaking and listening abilities had improved.

Looking deeper into the data revealed limitations to the linguistic expats' breadth of English competency. I found that linguistic expats selected areas of study based on their job roles and ignored areas of study that did not seem relevant. If their work required generating reports, they spent the majority of their study on writing skills while neglecting speaking skills. If their work called for absorbing written material, they spent the majority of their time developing vocabulary and reading abilities. If they were often called to interact with foreign coworkers, they invested in speaking skills.

Ultimately, the linguistic expats' efforts yielded partial language skills but were too narrow to produce advanced skills. Like a swimmer who has mastered only one stroke and therefore tires easily or a martial arts student who learns only two moves and is therefore easily overtaken by his opponent, linguistic expats remained stuck in what I call an interminable state of lingua franca *bounded fluency*. They acquired some degree of fluency, but it was insufficient to enable automaticity of the kind that native speakers develop. No matter how much they improved, they never achieved the natural ease of their fluent native language. Thus, whereas the vast majority of linguistic expats improved their grasp of English, they did not develop sufficient fluency to be able to relegate their lingua franca learning into the background. It remained an effortful foreground struggle. Where lingua franca was concerned, they were not "babbling" as the residents of the biblical city of Babel were said to do; nor were they able to hear and speak English with the miraculous clarity of those in the story who experienced the Pentecost.

BOUNDED FLUENCY AS A GLOBAL PHENOMENON

The fact that lingua franca bounded fluency is not unique to Rakuten, and is in fact widespread, makes it a phenomenon, one that poses a challenge for global collaboration and communication. Because English is the current lingua franca of global business, we would like to think that people will speak English with mastery and aplomb. Yet although employees advance in learning the lingua franca, and in their careers, they are likely to be limited by an environment that is unsuitable to mastering a foreign language. They do not necessarily have expert, native speakers to follow. I have found this to be true for linguistic expats whose native language is other than Japanese and in global companies where English as lingua franca has been in long-term use.

Another way to understand bounded fluency comes from the literature that has studied the discernable differences between being technically proficient in a language and being able to communicate in a way that truly fosters common understanding.[10] These studies hold that three types of language use exist in organizations: everyday language, company speak, and technical/industry language. Each of these language types involves a different set of linguistic and communications competencies—to achieve fluency in English would conceivably require the Rakuten employees to master all three competencies and be able to move easily back and forth between each one many times per day, sometimes even in the same sentence.[11]

One might think that achieving linguistic fluency in a foreign language is only a matter of practice and time, both of which were in relatively short supply for the Rakuten employees. Yet my findings from another in-depth lingua franca and globalization study suggest that bounded fluency is difficult to overcome and part of the expat perspective. I studied 115 linguistic expats who worked for WorldTech (pseudonym), a U.S.-based multinational technology company that had over 350,000 employees in 160 countries and had established English as its default lingua franca for global work for three decades. In this study, participants who worked in their home countries such as Brazil, China, France, Germany, Italy, Japan, Korea, Russia, Singapore, and Spain were asked to reflect on their experiences with language and cross-border leadership over time. The interviewees were senior managers in country, product, and service lines; vice presidents; managing directors; and chief operating officers. Their average tenure at WorldTech was twenty-two years and more than half of the interviewees (54 percent) had been on at least one international assignment. The average age of respondents was forty-nine; and 23 percent of the sample was female. Forty-six percent of the interviewees had participated in English language coaching at the request of WorldTech leadership.

Despite their extensive career progressions and tenure at World-Tech, I was struck to find that the vast majority of these leaders reported a continued struggle with their language capabilities similar to that of employees at Rakuten who were just beginning their migration to English as the lingua franca. Despite their struggles, these particular linguistic expats held positions where they managed other non-native speakers. Most had to make decisions and design strategies that enabled subordinates to improve their language capacity as well as prevent language issues from harming the bottom line of the business. Moreover, their roles required daily use of English to hold meetings where they were called upon to provide feedback, persuade, and negotiate.

In the next chapter we will take up the response to Englishnization by the second of the three groups at Rakuten I identified —U.S. employees—and named the cultural expats.

4

Cultural Expats and the Trojan Horse of Language

"IT'S THEIR CULTURE WRAPPED IN OUR LANGUAGE"

> Thank God he picked my language!
> —U.S. EXECUTIVE

> When a football game is about to start and you see a team about to run out to the field and they break through the banner and you see these guys running, that's the vision that you have when you think about Rakuten [HQ]. You think of these people coming, they're coming.
> —U.S. MANAGER

While the Tokyo employees were responding with fear, worry, and anxiety to Mikitani's 2010 Englishnization announcement, those in Boston, New York, and San Francisco were cheering with excitement and joyful anticipation. Robert was thrilled. "Being in the United States and having English as my first language puts me in an incredibly lucky position," he said, echoing the feeling of many native English-speaking subsidiary employees. Initially, the response to Englishnization was: "It's great for us here. We don't have to put in any work and we get all the benefits." As more than one self-congratulatory informant bluntly put it: "We've got that box checked." Robert explained that unlike their Japanese counterparts, who had to undertake a much more arduous path, for the native English speakers, the language mandate promised to bring positive changes without any cost. Little did he know that was only part of the story.

This chapter will follow the native English speakers through their first phase, when euphoria reigned because they (incorrectly, as it turned out) assumed that Englishnization was solely about language, and through the second phase, about two years into Englishnization, when they found it nearly as difficult to accept the changes wrought in their day-to-day workplace as did the native Japanese speakers. While the Japanese employees had to change to adopt a foreign language, the American employees had to change to adopt the Rakuten organizational culture that had been mostly suppressed by the language barrier. Employees in both groups had to adjust their perception of themselves and their place in the company—in this respect, the groups were mirror images of one another.

In their self-assurance during the first phase, some native English-speaking informants exhibited linguistic ethnocentricity, the idea that one party's way of using language or communicating takes precedence over another, often privileging the perspective of a native speaker.[1] Rather than understanding that English had become the lingua franca of choice for global work, some American native speakers assumed that it was *their* country, *their* culture, and *their* market that were of interest. As one forty-five-year-old executive in charge of operations reasoned:

> I think that everyone in the American [subsidiaries] recognizes that they picked *our* language. Everyone recognizes that there's a reason behind that and I feel that a message has resonated, whether spoken or not, that indicates that decision was made because this market is of tremendous importance; and I think that

I confidently know that if you talk to a lot of people and probe them on that front, they would come to the same conclusion.

Another native speaker, enabled by the lingua franca mandate to present directly to the CEO for the first time, echoed this sentiment, saying, "Rakuten, they need us. . . . And that's the presentation that I gave to [leaders in Japan]. I told them, 'If we execute here [in the United States], we can become bigger here." This confidence abounded in the U.S. offices, as further illustrated by this comment by technology specialist who had been with the company just a year:

> Just the fact that Rakuten is a Japanese company and we're a U.S. company is huge. I think it's funny how we in the United States typically look to foreign countries for help. Here, it's a parallel universe.

Cultural expats were prideful about their relative position in the company. As Alice (34), an engineer, attested, "We do have technology that everyone wants. And we pride ourselves on that. And everyone knows it." True, the U.S. market, its subsidiaries, and their technologies were important for Rakuten's global growth strategy. Leading e-commerce competitors, such as Amazon, eBay, and Yahoo, were based in the United States and Rakuten had formed a disproportionately high number of acquisitions there compared to other global markets in which they were engaged. However, their ethnocentric attitudes and failure to understand either the proper role for English as the lingua franca or the relativity of American cultural norms were all antithetical to the expat perspective.

In addition to the false sense of confidence and erroneous perspective that comes with ethnocentricity, in their naiveté, the cultural expats falsely assumed that culture must match up with language. Adopting the English language, they believed, also meant adopting the Westernized culture of native English speakers. For example, Dan, a U.S. salesperson, evidenced this sentiment when he said, "I mean these guys are learning English, and the American way." In other words, the American employees could not at first accommodate the idea that the English language could be a conduit of a foreign culture, or that omotenashi, described in chapter 2, could be a source of differentiation, one that Mikitani had emphasized constantly. These sentiments would change as the Japanese corporate culture, powered by English, was streamed into the U.S. subsidiaries. Eventually, the cultural air in the U.S. offices would change. As one interviewee would note, "I can't really explain it. The influence is very tangible when you're talking about it. It feels like another country's influence on America."

First Phase
IMPROVED COMMUNICATION

Although the Englishnization mandate did not make the Japanese Rakuten members fluent, their language skills did progress enough to make U.S. employees beneficiaries of improved communication. Individual employees had access to and interactions with more coworkers in Japan, especially once the circle of people with adequate proficiency began to grow. A U.S. accountant, who had worked at the company for over four years, described her experience before the mandate:

> I wouldn't necessarily understand their [the Japanese] requests just because of the way it was phrased, so I'd have to go back and ask for clarification. There's a little bit of back and forth there. Then it seems like certain documents and things I'd sent, I was asked for them again and again several times. I wasn't sure if there was a language issue . . . or if they were able to fully comprehend everything I'd sent. It was inefficient communication. It seemed very inefficient because I was repeating myself, asking for clarification, redoing what I'd already done.

Within a year of the mandate, she had a different perspective: "I think people all kind of feel the same way—it's better because we can communicate now, it's easier to communicate with people in Japan." The duration and the back-and-forth cycles that were customary to develop mutual understanding trimmed down because people had an easier time conveying and assimilating each other's basic information. These improvements enhanced the quality of cross-border work. However, as we will see later in this chapter, and as much of the literature shows, simply having a common language does not eliminate communication issues; organizational and national culture play an important role. An expat perspective means, in part, acknowledging that the interaction of language and culture must be considered.[2]

Despite the linguistic expats' struggle with bounded fluency, Englishnization enabled them to communicate better with the American subsidiary workforce; as a result, some work processes improved. For the first two years, the native English speakers could still believe that Englishnization would only make their work easier. For example, a native English-speaking IT support staff member who had worked in the New York office for roughly five years explained that prior to Englishnization, discerning and resolving an issue emanating from headquarters was always a protracted exercise. Much was lost in communication, and technical failures festered for days in the course of diagnosing the nature of the problem. Post-Englishnization, he was pleased by his ability to be more effective in his job because communication was smoother. He explained the shift:

> Englishnization has definitely reduced the turnaround time on not only getting questions and data and information back to [my counterpart in Japan] but also the turnaround time in closing out a ticket for that [counterpart in Japan]; doors have opened to us for resolution. We used to go back and forth for a few days before I even realized what the issue might be, whereas now we get a ticket, we pretty much know right away what their ask is.

Another employee who worked as an accountant reported on the improvements in his work life post-mandate. Previously, he had relied on his Japanese counterparts to serve his clients and had grappled with "getting e-mails in Japanese symbols." He was often frustrated and attempted to find ways to translate the "symbols" on his end, whether it was through the one bilingual colleague who worked in his area or using online translation tools to get a general idea of what the characters meant. Neither of these approaches was sufficient to clarify or confirm communiqués that often had meaningful client service implications. As a last resort, he said that he would often be forced to respond and "remind people that I don't speak Japanese, and they were always very apologetic." Englishnization afforded him faster and more accurate exchanges with the right people in Japan:

> I would say that I do communicate mostly via e-mail—actually 99 percent via e-mail—with more people now, and I understand that I can send an e-mail to anyone on the e-mail chain and for the most part they'll understand what I'm saying. It's made it easier. A lot easier . . . I notice just a bigger range of people able to communicate better and really making that effort to communicate even if there are challenges.

And a third example, although more problematic than the previous two, also evidences improved communication among American and Japanese workers. Mark (42), a software developer whose previous Rakuten experience included videoconferencing, relied on translators in the room (from Japan or the United States) during these meetings. Despite the enhanced communication cues inherent in video calling (facial expressions, gestures, tone of voice), three-way language communication had taken a long time and misinterpretation of technical information had not been unusual, primarily because translators were not technical experts.[3] As Mark said, "Translators don't necessarily have information and knowledge about the particular things that you're talking about."

Englishnization promised to remove some of those limitations, enabling people to have direct exchanges without the presence of language brokers. At first, however, setbacks occurred. Mark recalled that shortly after the mandate was implemented, the pace of work slowed down, which conflicted with one of Rakuten's principles of accomplishing work tasks rapidly:

> People really were trying their English, but something they could have said in five minutes took them twenty. Those were the lumps that we all had to take as listeners. We all had to just work through it

all, which was tough to do because one of the five commandments is "speed, speed, speed." So we're like, "Come on. Let's go, let's go!"

Within five months, Mark reported material differences in his engagement with Japanese employees on his videoconferences and his face-to-face conversations. When I met with Mark a year after Englishnization was instituted, he had just returned from a trip to Tokyo. The company was changing fast and he gleaned much more from his trip this time around than he had on previous trips. Despite the Japanese employees' self-perceived struggle to learn English and discomfort with using the language, Mark boldly ascribed 1000 percent success to Englishnization.

> I recently went to Rakuten in September, in Tokyo, and it was just amazing to see the progress and people speaking to me in English. And I think that trip was an incredible learning experience. I don't know if we would have learned as much had there been more of a language barrier. The fact that I went to Japan and saw it firsthand is what really drives me—having experienced what it is like to work with Rakuten prior to going through that, prior to Englishnization, and then having that trip, allows me to be able to say, "Yes, it's a 1000 percent success, in my opinion."

Speaking English directly, rather than through a translator, also gave native English speakers more nuanced knowledge of the true needs and functions of the organization and a greater understanding of how they fit into the workings of the firm overall. Such was the experience of another U.S.-based employee who had worked at Rakuten for three years and had previously relied on translators to communicate with colleagues in Japan.

> Whether it's client facing or whether it's internally, the English language helped bring us all together so that it's not a bunch of pieces moving independent of each other. We understand better how we can fit or what our role is in achieving that goal. Having the common language really helped us understand—in a way that translation wouldn't—where we fit into the larger picture.

Taken together, then, having a lingua franca afforded communication, tacit and explicit, in a way that went further than it had with translators. While translators could significantly aid two parties who did not have sufficient fluency to communicate directly, they were limited when it came to discerning and accurately conveying content that was profession specific, technical, or organization dependent.[4] When translators became obsolete at Rakuten, U.S.-based native speakers experienced a more expansive and direct connection with Japanese colleagues that eventually began to include some nuance and specificity.

ANTICIPATION OF CAREER ADVANCEMENT

Cultural expats' linguistic ethnocentrism trapped them into expecting the language mandate would lead to open-ended and enduring sources of opportunities for career growth. They believed that impending opportunities would allow them to reap the rewards of their (newly) heightened status, as well as to better serve the needs of the greater organization. In particular, many individuals expressed optimism about taking on new, attractive, and globally oriented assignments across Rakuten.[5]

In the era before the lingua franca, many had viewed their inability to speak the company's main language, Japanese, as a constant disadvantage, but the company's adoption of English changed language as a limiting factor. As one employee expressed:

> Without [the mandate], being able to evolve inside [Rakuten] wouldn't be possible. I'd probably look for outside opportunities to grow my career. Now, I can move around and work with other groups, getting positions that are open to me. So for me, it's great. Switching to English definitely opened up opportunities for my career path.

Thus native English speakers pictured themselves taking advantage of new career choices. A product manager noted of the mandate, "It could expand opportunities. If this wasn't an English [speaking] company, it would be hard to visualize myself working in other countries."

Moreover, native English speakers' career expectations rose when they witnessed members of their subsidiary taking on company-wide leadership positions. A director of an engineering group expressed his enthusiasm about a colleague's new assignment in terms that suggest impending and increased status gains for his social group: "You will actually have an American who is going over there [to Japan] to take over! That's totally amazing." Another employee described a colleague's advancement similarly: "His role has expanded. He's not just doing work for the [U.S. subsidiary] but for the entire company as a whole, even other locations overseas." The advances of peers were seen as a palpable marker of the overall potential for personal career movement and as confirmation of the native English speakers' heightened capacity to, if not "take over," at least contribute to the firm.

A marketing executive's response was emblematic of this belief: "I think you become more valuable. Imagine the next time [Rakuten] enters another country where English is not the first language, but they speak English." Fluency in the lingua franca was perceived as a fundamental qualifier for employees' contributions as the company entered new regions. The following quote from a business analyst portrays this dynamic—wherein the ability to add value melds with the acceptance of greater professional opportunities:

> I anticipate that there will be more growth . . . [and] lots of opportunities for people to do interesting non-U.S. work integrating new businesses into the company. . . . And I think there will be people here [in the United States] that will be excited about that opportunity.

It is clear that following the language mandate, American employee-informants believed that they possessed an enhanced ability to contribute to their greater organization. Whether their contribution involved serving in existing subsidiary locations or aiding the integration of future acquisitions, a majority of informants anticipated that this increased professional value would advance their careers.

Second Phase

LANGUAGE AS CULTURAL CARRIER: THE TROJAN HORSE OF LANGUAGE

Two years into Englishnization, the native English speakers at Rakuten had a very different story to tell. Their euphoric anticipation of career advancement—status hikes with minimal effort and larger contributions to the organization—was proving illusory. Instead, as they became inundated with Rakuten's corporate culture, which was steeped in Japanese cultural traditions, as well as new demands from the Tokyo headquarters, their position in the company shifted to one they found, at least at first, unsettling and uprooting.

Like the radical Englishnization implementation strategy in Japan, which was immediate and across the board, the second phase of Englishnization in the American subsidiaries was implemented without a gradual rollout or pilot study group. One day a massive, encyclopedic-like policy handbook arrived in the U.S. Rakuten offices. Employees were as astonished by the handbook's size as they were by its very existence, which had been previously unknown. Though the book had long been a fixture in the Tokyo headquarters, Englishnization had recently enabled its translation from Japanese.

Although rule-setting and standardization of work processes are often inevitable consequences of an organization's globalizing expansion, this had decidedly *not* been the case with Rakuten, where some of the subsidiaries were acquired years before Englishnization and therefore continued operating more or less autonomously. The handbook painstakingly documented the organizational culture, that is, the values, norms, and expected behaviors for a Rakuten employee. Guidelines ranged from the required placement of name badges to specific ways to demonstrate the Rakuten principles. As a marketing specialist described it: "The handbook is like a code, a corporate code. . . . It's a way of conducting yourself and a corporate set of rules to abide by." Another American expressed that the handbook made her feel like headquarters was "indoctrinating us with their Rakutenness."

For many U.S. employees, the unilateral process by which the sudden and complete installation of the Rakuten corporate culture was implemented was as bewildering as, if not more so than, the daily work changes themselves. In this regard, the cultural expats' experience of sudden "shock" and "identity threat" was equivalent to that of the linguistic expats.

The American employees experienced culture shock. Although the native English speakers did not have to change to a foreign language when stepping from the street to their place of employment (as did native-speaking, Japan-based employees who experienced language shock), the mandate forced a change to a foreign way of thinking and behaving inside the organization, making them belong to a category I conceptualized as "cultural expats."

Nearly overnight, cultural expats realized that their initial enthusiasm had given them a false sense of security. They were entirely naïve to the fact that while previous language barriers had shielded them from the Tokyo headquarters' frequent demands, the lingua franca adoption enabled Japanese managers to develop sufficient fluency to translate materials into English that called for substantive changes.

I call this phenomenon the Trojan Horse of Language. Like the enormous wooden horse that the ancient Greeks gifted the city of Troy that hid warriors who opened the city gates to the encroaching Greek army, the "gift" of English that the U.S. employees greeted so ecstatically at the outset in fact carried something more difficult to fathom, namely, a foreign corporate culture.[6] The U.S. employees had thought that the English language mandate would Westernize work practices and work values, that is, their native culture, but in reality the opposite happened: Englishnization transmitted Rakuten's Japanese work practices and values.

Several factors accounted for their surprise. First, had the U.S. employees not harbored so many inflated expectations and such unquestioned linguistic ethnocentricity, the force with which Rakuten's culture arrived might have been less surprising and they might have been better prepared for the challenges and conflicts it would bring. Second, prior to Englishnization, most non-Japanese employees had unwittingly held an incomplete view of Rakuten's espoused values and norms because language barriers had prevented a significant portion of the company's culture and practices from making the voyage across continents. Third, logistically, the Japanese employees' initial difficulties in learning English delayed the subsidiaries' culture shock for as many as two years. Not until they became aware of Rakuten's culture and work practice expectations did people actually experience anxiety regarding the loss of familiar signs and symbols that had allowed them to orient in cross-cultural contexts. Much like their mirror images, the linguistic expats, feelings of loss and anxiety ultimately made up the core of the cultural expats' experience.[7]

WORK PRACTICES AND WORK VALUES

In the second round of interviews with the cultural expats, I found a marked difference in their responses than I had in the first round. This time, people discussed cultural differences, newly emphasizing reporting to management and management's desire for data; differences in Japanese versus U.S. work ethics and social customs; whether communication was direct or indirect; and the fact that the policy handbook pushed principles from the top down. Prior to Englishnization, it seemed these concerns were absent, or at least present to a lesser degree, and therefore the cultural expats had reckoned very little with them. These concerns largely fell into two categories: the changes in daily work practices and the changes in the way they were expected to think about their work.

Task-Based Processes

Task-based process changes were the most obvious in the second phase: these included website design; performance management systems, such as key performance indicators (KPI); and reports or general company-wide routines, such as the Asakai meetings. As they transitioned toward more formalized, regimented work practices, these process changes impacted U.S. employees' daily work practices. Even more important, these changes in work practice routines shifted the expectations for the American subsidiaries away from their former Westernized culture with its emphasis on the individual to the stricter, striving, group-oriented Japanese culture.

While meetings and reports had always been part of task-based processes, post-Englishnization they increased in frequency and intensity. An engineer who had been with the company for a little over three years spoke to the tremendous process shift that had occurred:

> There's a huge culture shock. . . . Now, we're at a process-oriented state where everything is dictated by due diligence, by KPI management. . . . The Japanese culture is a manufacturing culture; it is very, very process-driven. . . . So we had to go through an evolution and an education here.

A major post-mandate process change was that work groups were required to report KPIs, which enabled Rakuten to create a strict information system to control an otherwise far-flung global organization. And this information was siphoned up to headquarters through large-scale reporting efforts, involving human touch points throughout the organization that worked on a weekly or even daily basis to update their managers. Two years after the mandate, one Boston staff member resented the close control as "hovering."

> They [Rakuten headquarters] sit over you and watch everything you do. A lot of reporting. They want to know daily what's going on . . . I've worked at large companies and I've not seen this hovering type of thing, you know, constantly reporting over and over and over again on a daily basis, just the new numbers from one day to the next.

Many employees intimately felt the impact of these new routines and processes in their daily lives within the subsidiaries, and some resented the changes.

A manager who had been in the high-tech industry for over a decade explained the changes he observed—including the scoring and corresponding monitoring mechanisms—and how difficult it was to conform to these new rules:

than feeling the Rakuten culture and practices as a burdensome weight, they exhibited what I label "positive indifference." Indifference because they possessed the goodwill and ability to shrug off the weight of the cultural elements and to engage them with limited concern. Positive because in regards to the mandate's changes, their indifference was a desirable attribute, one that helped ease their transition. Although positive indifference is similar to aspects of cultural acceptance and tolerance, a distinction exists. While acceptance or tolerance implies that some degree of resistance to cultural difference must be overcome, positive indifference overlooks cultural differences as not especially important or worthy of attention while remaining optimistic about the process of engaging the culture seen as foreign.

The concept of positive indifference was captured by Bernard, a German interviewee, who described his response to the new rule about wearing the badge: "Personally, it didn't bother me. . . . It wasn't a question of agreeing or disagreeing with it." The key word here is "personally." Bernard could observe the new rule without it acquiring in his mind a threat to his personal identity; for him, it was just a new rule rather than a cultural difference he had to expend energy learning to tolerate. His neutrality was, in this situation, a positive development. Dual expats could easily take on a positive (or neutral) position vis-à-vis cultural differences, in part because they were able to see differences in language or culture as superficial changes rather than as substantial impediments, even if what they were asked to do did not make immediate or complete sense.

Positive indifference did not preclude the dual expats from noticing or having opinions about unfamiliar challenges in work practices and approaches required by their parent company once the English mandate took effect. A customer service manager, despite admitting to this pressure, spoke positively of the Japanese demands: "The pressure I am under is part of the normalization of work. It is stimulating. It is a challenge. It is a pleasant pressure." They learned that Japanese colleagues were likely to tackle a problem by first analyzing all the different angles and issues, while the French admitted that their approach was to attack a problem "kamikaze style," head-on. They acknowledged that while the French strategy might be more efficient in terms of time than the Japanese strategy, it might also be less effective. Their creative use of a Japanese word as a metaphor for a French characteristic is evidence of the kind of freedom and receptivity that dual expats experienced. When some of the German and Indonesian dual expats chose to wear kimonos at regional conferences, they again demonstrated a creative acceptance and even a willingness to embrace the Japanese cultural infusion as a positive change.

The required ID badge with the five Rakuten principles that so many cultural expats found difficult provoked a more or less indifferent reaction in dual expats, even if they did not altogether see its value. Others referred to previous experiences where they had to wear name badges (e.g., "I did have to wear one at another company"). Overall, they were open to trying it and it did not cause any troublesome emotions. Celine from the French office explained her perspective in which she characterized the demands from the corporate headquarters as inconsequential: "And what has been added is the Monday morning meeting, wearing a name tag, and miscellaneous small changes . . . I'm indifferent to it. . . . Once it's there, we forget about it."

Bernard, who initially described his indifference to the badge, in the course of the interview found justifications for how it could yield positive results for a growing company. In his words:

> I'm very neutral about it, but I don't think it is something very useful. They said it was for security reasons that we had to wear a badge, but we only wear it once we are at work. It's true that it can maybe be useful when you meet somebody you don't know, seeing how fast the company is growing.

"It's not so serious," explained Alfred (32), a German interviewee who enumerated the series of norms and rules that were instituted, even though such practices were novel for him as someone who had spent his career to date working in the technology sector in Germany. Alfred's coworker found the onslaught of values enacted by Rakuten overly "pedantic." But like Alfred, he trivialized their significance: "I do not put a lot of importance on that."

Asakai meetings and the policy handbook with meticulously documented guidelines were also obvious changes for all dual expats. Here, too, they found ways to appreciate difference. A content developer from France gave his opinion:

[The Rakuten culture] is more ceremonial [than French culture]. . . . Every Monday we have the Asakai, and there are more things that you have to strictly follow. . . . More rules. More exchanges. When we send an e-mail we have to add more people in copy. It doesn't complicate things. I think it is a beneficial thing; for example, we have more info on how the company is doing, we feel more involved . . . I think it is important. We feel we are part of a big family. We have family meetings. The fact of wearing a badge is important so that we know who we are talking to.

Dual expats' ability to engage in positive indifference contributed to both their sense of security and, correspondingly, their lack of an identity threat. A forty-five-year-old Japanese manager charged in part with managing Rakuten's European operations explained, "The French are doing really well. They see the good and bad points of the 'Japanese way' and they integrate their [French] ways, so it happens naturally. They're adapting." Unlike the cultural expats who eventually rebelled against the source of their own identity threat—the Trojan Horse and cultural infusion from Japan—the dual expats experienced a natural progression. Integration happened without the bitterness and frustration experienced in the United States.

A client engagement representative from Brazil expressed her excitement about working for Rakuten:

I like to always develop . . . to grow . . . I think in a Japanese company you are expected to not stay where you are. You have to find new things day-to-day, to understand new things, to search for more knowledge and I think that's something awesome about a Japanese company . . . I would say that it [Japanese culture] doesn't affect me. In a negative way it doesn't. I think it is really good and everybody is adapting and following the way.

She realized the positive benefits of being in a Japanese company, where she would be greeted with novel experiences and pushed to adapt and grow as a person. Like other dual expats across Rakuten's global offices who exhibited positive indifference, she was impervious to the perceived harm felt by her linguistic expat and cultural expat colleagues who experienced identity threats.

Seeking Commonality

While some of the cultural expats perceived differences between their native culture and a foreign one as negative and repellent, dual expats displayed a willingness to find commonalities between the two cultures that could draw them closer. In the same way that Inga, whom we met at the beginning of this chapter, was able to find common ground between German and Japanese regard for rules and hard work, finding a commonality enables one to draw closer to the foreign culture and become receptive to its differences. Interestingly, the aspect of Japanese culture with which natives chose to identify varied according to nationality.

Bhoddi, a Thai interviewee, traveled to Tokyo for manager training sessions that emphasized the five shugi principles at the basis of Rakuten's corporate culture. A devout Buddhist, Bhoddi extrapolated commonalities between Buddhist principles/principles of the Buddha and Rakuten's shugi, suggesting that the Japanese were not the first to come up with the concept of five principles and that both the shugi and Buddhism stressed that the five principles must coexist.

When discussing the Rakuten cultural values, a linguistic-cultural expat from Brazil spoke about omotenashi as one of the Eastern concepts that he identified with personally. He found commonality with omotenashi, the inherent emphasis on caring for others, while also acknowledging the stringent realities of producing rigorous measurable results:

> I identify with Rakuten's philosophy a lot. They focus a lot on the people, they have this concept that is hard to translate into Portuguese, which is the omotenashi, a server's soul. . . . You

really worry about attending to the other person as if he were a close, good comrade of yours. And I really like that; I think that humanizes a little the work atmosphere even though there are a lot of goals and numbers. It is always metrics, measurements, and numbers all the time, but you can feel that there is a more human part within the company, I think that at least for me that makes all the difference.

And an accountant in Germany sought commonality by focusing on the natural progression between the local ways of working and those newly introduced by Rakuten:

I feel like much of that is introduced was already in place in Germany but by another name. It wasn't explicitly formulated. "Speed, speed, speed," for instance, we already had that. There is no difference, it was like that before. But now it is written down as a rule. Then you explain to your coworker: "We've done that for the past five years, and that's the reason we are where we are! It's nice that the Japanese realized that too!" . . . It's clear, it's common sense. . . . Normal stuff! So, someone included it in a philosophy. And we abide by it. It is okay. But actually, we already do it that way, and we do it because it is something that we believe in.

A French engineer highlighted a number of commonalities that were salient to him between French and Japanese culture:

I think that the fact that we [France and Japan] have exactly the same way of working—that we're very focused on results, that we're rigorous and professional, that we put our means where they're necessary and not elsewhere, that we always analyze everything we do to find axes of improvement. . . . It makes it such that, even when there are cultural differences, if we have the same way of working, it will work out well.

The search for commonality was also reflected in the narrative of the following Indonesian consultant, who compared Rakuten's ritual of asking employees to clean their work area for five minutes weekly with his religious practice.

I'll give you one example. Like [desk] cleaning. . . . Say for instance most of the people, 90 percent of the population [in In-
donesia], are Muslim. So I said, "Hey, when you go to mosque,
you wash your hands, wash your feet. Exact same concept. It's
like work. Work is more like you have to commit. And then this
is your place. And that's why you are responsible."

In sum, dual expats displayed an interest to grow and develop in
new and unexpected ways as a result of Englishnization and found
positive ways to connect with cultural aspects of the Rakuten way.
The dual expats, like the cultural expats, were required to adopt the
new and stricter work practices imported from the Japanese headquarters, but the dual expats were capable of realizing the benefits of
such practices—namely, that they allow for action either to improve
processes (kaizen) or to preempt issues. Dual expats were also able to
find common ground that drew their ways of working together instead
of apart. This continuity and commonality between the old ways of the
local subsidiary and the new ways of the parent organization helped
dual expats accept the changes taking place around them and seemed
to further buffer them from the experience of identity threats.

Identifying with a Global Organization

Lingua franca adoption can have mixed outcomes in terms of how
individual workers perceive their relationship with the employer organization. Language can influence whether people see themselves
as inside or outside a group.[13] Some research has shown that learning
the common language increases individual perceptions of belonging
and connection with the organization and serves as a reminder that
the organization has a global vision.[14] Certainly that was the case
with the dual expats at Rakuten.

The sense of being inside an organization, or experiencing one-
ness with a company, known as organizational identification,[15] enabled dual expats to identify with Rakuten as a global enterprise.
Employees typically emphasized their sense of belonging to a dynamic global group where they felt information is shared, people
are valued, and the strategy is very clear. Around the world, dual ex-

pats melded their individual identity with the company as a global enterprise and saw themselves as part of its globalization process. An Indonesian interviewee noted his intention that his work be aligned with the global effort: "Because from my perspective, if I'm doing my job, I'm becoming part of the globalization of the company." Individual identity, in his mind, was synonymous with the collective global company and its further expansion.

Moreover, dual expats felt that they embodied the global company's identity and were its representatives. A German e-commerce specialist remarked, "I can definitely identify myself with the company. And I also support the decisions that are made in Japan and can represent this accordingly." A manager in Taiwan spoke of his pride in belonging to a larger successful global group.

> I'd say it's primarily a source of pride, in the sense of belonging to a global company that has not only grown but is part of a larger group. Then, the fact that it's Japanese, it's perhaps an even greater source of pride—the Japanese model is so successful.

Cultural or national differences did not impede the ability to adopt a global superordinate identity, as one might expect, but rather hastened it along. Dual expats' sense of belonging to a single, united organization was a further extension of their capacity to see difference as positive and find commonality. In fact, global organizational identification was made possible through the increased feelings of connectedness brought about by a common, accessible language. Dual expats were quick to realize not only that the influx in information sharing and communicating was a strategy but that each person's role in the larger picture was a hallmark of the lingua franca movement.

Global organizational identification was also driven from the top down in the form of explicit messaging from Rakuten headquarters. It featured prominently in the CEO's frequent messaging. An Indonesian business analyst attested: "I think it's a global company. It's on Hiroshi Mikitani's mind every week during Asakai. He makes the global company always stay on my mind-set." The company's efforts to globalize were prominent for all of Rakuten's linguistic-cultural expat employees in ways they were not for the other two groups. In Brazil, the tangible sense of being global was ever-present in informants' work lives, from the Japanese CEO's messaging to the Japanese expats that the Brazilians worked alongside:

> Our Asakai starts with a video of the CEO in English . . . and it's a palpable reminder that you are in one global company. Then you have interactions in English, or you see a guy from Japan speaking in English, you think. . . . Yeah, I am global.

Employees across all of Rakuten's subsidiaries were constantly reminded of Rakuten's globalization efforts. Identifying with a global organization thus became a foundational component of dual expats' global work orientation. Without it, employees might be perceived as lacking a crucial organizational characteristic by which they could prove themselves and improve their position within the company. By melding their individual or local identity into the collective, global organization, dual expats avoided any sense of threatened identity. Instead, these identities were one and the same. "For me, it's interesting to be a subsidiary of an international group," a French staff assistant affirmed. "It's interesting, it's positive. . . . To be honest . . . I'm happy to come into the office every morning."

Aspiring to Global Careers

Another component of dual expats' global work orientation was a deep desire to serve in a global job role, inside or outside of the company. Some interviewees had preexisting ambitions to work globally, while others' dreams had been kindled by Rakuten's Englishnization, as well as by its global growth and reach. Many hoped to undertake a global career because they expected that such a path would be replete with opportunities to grow professionally. These ambitions were also tied with Rakuten's globalization efforts and its stated goal to become the "number one Internet company in the world."

Especially after the lingua franca mandate was introduced, these dreams became realizable ambitions that were openly discussed. A Thai employee who was interviewed post-mandate was quick to suggest, "I dream that I'll go abroad someday. So I prepare myself with English." A French quality control analyst, also interviewed post-mandate, spoke of a possible future: "The opportunity I can see is to be transferred abroad, not necessarily to Japan, as well as the opportunity for [global] business travel."

Dual expats hoped that improving their proficiency in the lingua franca, combined with a parent company set on globalization, would improve their long-term global career trajectory overall. Including a line in their résumé that said "English speaking" would, they knew, boost their appeal as future job candidates. The potential to live and work abroad was very enticing to many employees regardless of their current location. Some even professed that their global career aspirations had led them to apply for a job at Rakuten. A recent hire from Brazil said: "I had just returned from Canada. I wanted to keep improving [my English] . . . and I was thinking of moving abroad . . . then I saw this opportunity."

A Taiwanese marketing specialist who had been with the company for over six years looked forward to the day when his hard work in learning English would pay off in a global opportunity: "It'll be great for me to have the chance to go to another country, to work in another country. It's definitely something I want to do in the future— when my English is better." Other dual expats wanted to jump into an international role for the very purpose of refining their English skills, as another Taiwanese employee who desired a global assignment expressed: "I just really want to have a job which can let me speak English every day." Regardless of the country in which they originated or lived, Englishnization presented not only an opportunity for personal growth but also a key to unlock possibilities they could only dream of beforehand.

Seeking Global Interactions
Dual expats' immediate workdays were transformed by manifold interactions with employees at other Rakuten locations. Unlike employees from the other two groups, who merely tolerated necessary contact with employees from other locations, the dual expats regularly sought out such interactions. Rakuten employees were engaged in a twenty-four-hour work cycle spanning the world from Europe to

South America and Southeast Asia. Yet employees in each of these locations, even when intimately tied to their individual markets, were far from isolated. The extent of voluntary interactions with other subsidiaries reported by each subsidiary was as follows: Brazil, 51.7 percent; France, 25 percent; Germany, 10.7 percent; Indonesia, 15.8 percent; Taiwan, 15.4 percent; and Thailand, 30.8 percent. These numbers were significantly higher than that calculated for the cultural expats' voluntary interactions with other subsidiaries, which hovered around 2 percent.[16]

Rakuten dual expats' experiences were in keeping with research findings that when interactions are high, there is a greater ability to develop trust and shared vision among international coworkers.[17] Their interactions were vital for knowledge sharing across sites. One Taiwanese business development manager explained the advantage of these engagements:

> In the videoconference, there are maybe ten different countries that come together for the global marketing meeting. So there's a lot of people on the screen . . . I think that it's good for me and my members. I tell them it's a good chance to learn something from different countries, because usually we run the business locally. . . . How do you know someone did very well in France, Japan, Thailand, or other countries? For example, last time France shared what they did for [a campaign]. . . . Then we know that Japan did this very well, so they ask other subsidiaries to do the same thing. We tried to copy Japan and so far it's good, but I heard that France had very good success and then they shared it with everyone. It proves that not only Japan can do that.

In other words, dual expats' ability to communicate directly with others across linguistic and cultural boundaries allowed tacit knowledge to become more explicit within the organization.[18] They realized that sharing information or best practices with peers in other subsidiary locations could be advantageous to their own markets. Often initially encouraged by headquarters, colleagues in similar functions around the globe would come together on their own to harness the knowledge resources that the broader company offered. Subsidiaries that faced similar challenges and opportunities shared common experiences that other, dissimilar subsidiaries or headquarters might not find relevant. A Thai informant discussing the implications of the rapidly expanding Internet business in his country pointed this out: "Learning from other countries, especially other developing countries, is very, very key. So that means I have to learn English to communicate." Implicit in his comment is that issues the Thai subsidiary faced might not necessarily align with those of the more developed American or French markets. Similarly, more advanced markets or more mature subsidiary companies such as those in the United States might not find it as relevant to initiate interactions with less developed sister companies.

In Germany, for example, informants reported frequent contact with the subsidiary in neighboring France. With a similar time zone and a shared Western European local market base, it was relatively easy for France and Germany to initiate frequent engagements. As a German linguistic-cultural expat said, "With the colleagues in Europe, there's more of a knowledge exchange." He elaborated on how these self-initiated interactions were often beneficial:

> Our team talks with people in France at least once a month. Sometimes you are just asking how business is going, or if you want to [get] advice regarding a specific topic . . . for example, the [another subsidiary] requested some telephone conferences because they have to shift their business model completely from the first-party sales model that they have at the moment to a third-party sales.

Dual expats' more frequent interaction across subsidiaries was an important indicator of their global work orientation. Unlike the cultural expats in the U.S. subsidiaries who believed, at first, that their superior language knowledge itself was sufficient for their jobs, or the linguistic expats in Tokyo who at first struggled with learning English, dual expats actively sought more global interactions and reaped the benefits of this added contact.

In addition to this blossoming of cross-subsidiary interactions, subsidiaries had become accustomed to interactions with Tokyo headquarters from their time of acquisition. After the mandate, the frequency of these interactions was unequivocal; 74 percent of dual expats reported regular interactions with their headquarters-based colleagues. Headquarters' policy of setting organizational priorities and monitoring each subsidiary's performance helped ensure frequent interactions, particularly in cases where the subsidiary had significant room to transform (i.e., mature). For example, dual expats in Brazil (97 percent) and from the Asian subsidiaries of Taiwan, Thailand, and Indonesia (86 percent), all of whom were eager to mature, were significantly more likely to report interactions with headquarters than their French and German counterparts (63 percent), who were farther along in maturation. A Taiwanese marketing manager discussed his frequent contact with Tokyo as they guided him during the post-implementation phase of a new customer relationship management (CRM) system:

> We are just learning this system and only have the handbook, so I am in constant contact with them because I want to know how they use it. . . . We didn't know how, why, all the details. I want to know more of the details, since they have a team to manage the system and in Taiwan, we don't have anyone to manage it.

While contact between Tokyo and Taiwan was initiated by headquarters, the subsidiary informant was quick to realize the potential benefit of his headquarters colleagues' knowledge about the new CRM technology. Rather than trudging through another routine interaction with headquarters, he became motivated to take advantage of an opportunity to learn "all the details" and later utilize them for his own benefit. Once these subsidiary-Tokyo interactions were under way, dual expats' eyes opened to the inherent new opportunities and advantages that were available globally.

Rising above Resistance to Cultural Change

Unlike the Japanese linguistic expats who aligned with Hofstede's notion of Japan as a collectivistic culture, or the American cultural expats who aligned with his notion of the United States as an individualistic culture, dual expats were from a mix of individualistic

icans, become cultural expats when they discover new constraints as the Japanese realize English language fluency as a vehicle for imposing Japanese corporate culture. The Japanese linguistic expats, who were most fearful professionally at the start, discover newfound opportunities and responsibilities as they gain fluency. Those we assume would fare best—bilingual workers—ended up faring worst because their services become obsolete.

In writing this book, I set out to deepen our understanding of and empathy for the lived experiences and challenges each of these groups endure when they must work in a non-native language, culture, or both. By capturing the experiences, thoughts, and feelings of employees and survey participants over the course of five years, my hope is that scholars and practitioners will take into account the complexities involved in tasking workers to adopt a language and to operate in a global organization. The presence of a lingua franca has profound implications for individuals and groups in global organizations. Not only does it demand that non-native speakers rely on self-learning for improving language skills, but it also challenges people to move beyond their cultural constraints. Employees, whether they begin the lingua franca journey as native speakers, native cultural adherents, or both, will experience a shift in their everyday reality. In addition, a one-language organization enables greater collaboration across national boundaries. It reshapes the makeup of an organization as new foreign entrants join the environment once an accessible common language exists. It even challenges the leadership approach of the most seasoned employees. For all these reasons and many more, it is crucial to continue empirical inquiry into the lingua franca phenomenon at the global workplace.

Like all studies, my research approach limits the type of claims that I can make. My choice to primarily collect and analyze qualitative data to capture employee experiences, by definition, limits my ability to make causal connections. For example, my approach does not support comparisons between the influence of language and culture changes and the influence of other organizational changes that result from global expansion through acquisitions. Similarly, in the absence of comparable cases, it is difficult to untangle the impact that stems from dynamics between headquarters and subsidiaries, acquirer and acquired, and on the other hand, the impact that stems from language and cultural dynamics. Comparisons and connections of this type are ripe for future research.

My focus on language and culture offers several useful insights to the cross-border acquisitions domain. For instance, my findings suggest that an acquisition does not automatically and immediately confer language and cultural changes on the acquired organization. At Rakuten, in some cases, subsidiaries that had been acquired seven years prior to the infusion of the lingua franca had continued to operate in a language and culture set apart from those of the headquarters. It was only after the firm instituted the single-language policy that its espoused culture began to spread across the subsidiaries. In addition, linguistic expats experienced a decline in their status as they grappled with learning a new language. This language-based diminution of status runs contrary to the relatively higher hierarchical rank that is often conferred to members of an organization's headquarters. Findings such as these can bring into sharp relief global workers' otherwise overlooked experiences and challenges in both headquarters and subsidiary locations.

At the organizational level, a lingua franca can be a decoupling force between language and culture, and has the capacity to redistribute influence through a company in unforeseen ways. Most notably, an English-speaking Western culture is not necessarily always dominant in globalized organizations. An e-commerce giant like Rakuten that hails from an island country can forcefully assert its cultural identity. Of course, Rakuten's journey is still in process and we do not know where it might lead. This study represents only a portion of what we can expect longitudinally when a globalizing organization makes a fundamental change to its official language. Additional research can uncover the next phases of the organization's global evolution.

Finally, my hope is that globalization, as it continues to be facilitated by language, can become not only a tool for economic expansion and exportation of the home culture but also a tool for greater empathy. The underlying urges that drive organizations to pursue opportunity, to secure a sustainable economic future back home, and to expand, capture, and export goods and culture all need to be complemented with fundamental empathy, self-learning, collaboration, and transformation.

ACKNOWLEDGMENTS

A large and diverse community shaped the ideas in this book. My interest in large-scale global projects can be traced back to Pam Hinds, who took me on my first research journey when I was a student at Stanford University. Along with Bob Sutton and Steve Barley, Pam fostered a vibrant intellectual space for me to explore the issues of language and global work. At a time when such issues were barely theorized in the organizational behavior field, and were not the safest path for a scholar-in-training to take on, they were extraordinary early mentors who continue to lend support and insight. I am deeply grateful to all three for believing in the importance and possibility of this work when it was no more than a seed.

My heartfelt gratitude goes to my team of bilingual researchers from the various HBS Global Research Centers (Europe, Japan, and Latin America) who worked with me closely to collect data for this book meticulously. Most important, they were my teachers and coaches when it came to understanding the local contexts that I was studying. I am also grateful to my Boston-based team, current and former: Tom Barrow, Kelly Basile, Alex Kayyal (HBS '11), Marina Miloslavsky, Nathan Overmeyer, Steven Shafer, and Ben Shamash (HBS '11), who were indispensable in advancing this work.

I am deeply grateful to Elaine Backman for helping me talk through emerging theories and frameworks and for providing very insightful comments on several versions of the work-in-progress. I wish to thank Jean Bartunek for also reading an early draft of the manuscript, encouraging me, and steering me in the right direction. I am grateful to Paul Leonardi for being an amazing friend who gave his insights along the way.

This book has improved immensely from the invaluable contributions of my Harvard Business School colleagues: Robin Ely, Linda Hill, Jay Lorsch, Joshua Margolis, Tony Mayo, and Leslie Perlow. Jay Lorsch, who was the first person to encourage me to write this book, always reminded to analyze the global organization as a system. Robin and Linda scrutinized the manuscript line by line more than once. They provided crucial feedback and always made themselves available when I reached out to obsess over anything that was in process. Their generosity humbles me. What I learned from them will last me a lifetime.

I am also very thankful to colleagues, current and former, who have helped me think through the material that formed the basis of this book, especially Michel Anteby, Julie Battilana, Ethan Bernstein, Bill George, Boris Groysberg, Ranjay Gulati, Rob Kaplan, Chris Marquis, Gautam Mukunda, Jeffrey Polzer, Ryan Raffaelli, Lakshmi Ramarajan, and Scott Snook.

I am deeply appreciative to Harvard Business School for the generous financial support of this resource-intensive endeavor.

I am grateful to Karen Propp for her outstanding editorial support every step of the way. I couldn't have asked for a more patient and skilled partner. I wish to thank Meagan Levinson and Princeton University Press for helping me realize the substance and spirit of this work. I am also very appreciative to the anonymous reviewers whose insightful comments have helped sharpen the book's overarching frame, concepts, and presentation.

I wish to thank Frankie and Angie Rance for making FDR in Jamaica my family's home away from home, where many pages of this book were written.

I have always benefited from parents who supported my various endeavors unconditionally. Producing this book was no different. I am grateful for their sustained encouragement through the ups and downs. In word and deed, they have modeled perseverance in the face of uncertainty. My mother's frequent refrain, "Go all out and *yemeta yemta*!" is forever engraved in my mind.

My husband, Lawrence, and I sat side-by-side at cafés all over the Bay area for a year writing our respective doctoral dissertations.

Little did we know then that we would still be immersed in the same subjects a decade later. I couldn't ask for a better emotional and intellectual partner to walk with me through every phase of this project: discovering the twists and turns that language created in the field, the time I felt stared down by thousands of pages of data, my tenth rewrite of a chapter that never made the final cut, the countless hours spent talking through budding concepts, and the joy when the framework emerged as if it had always existed, undeniable. If Lawrence's intellectual support were not enough, I am very thankful for how he created the conditions for me to work freely on weekends and evenings while ensuring that our two young sons—Gabe and Daniel—continued to feel whole.

At the ages of six and four, Gabe and Daniel have learned to endure my absences while I traveled extensively. I am sure my trips away from them, in my role as a global field scholar, seemed as endless to them as it did to me. Still, the many people in the various countries I encountered during those trips have indirectly gifted them with exposure to the vastness of the world beyond their yards. Their global curiosity has been piqued, just as mine was piqued by my parents when I was their age. Gabe and Daniel's contribution to this book came forcefully toward the end. Wanting to test if the title, *The Language of Global Success*, would "stick," I shared it with them once and then asked them to repeat it several times from memory. When they remembered it again and again over a period of twenty-four hours, I knew that we had finally landed on the right title.

I finally turn to the many current and former Rakuten employees who generously opened their worlds to me. I am grateful beyond words for their willingness to share their experiences, insights, questions, fears, and hopes. As I started to draft the manuscript, I relied heavily on a number of people around the globe to get the contextual factors right. This was particularly important because the company's global expansion was rapid during the period of my study. I am deeply thankful to cofounders Masatada "Seichu" Kobayashi and Akio Sugihara for their passion and insights along the way. Kyle Yee, who led the Englishnization implementation, and Koichi Noda have been invaluable in helping me understand the complex ecosystem and organizational culture that formed the Rakuten way.

This book would not have been possible without Hiroshi Mikitani's willingness to let me fully "enter" his organization. I will forever be grateful that he trusted me to study and write about Rakuten without imposing a single condition. Mikitani has always expressed a desire to make his company a role model for the betterment of Japanese society and the wider world. He has always wanted others to learn from his experiences, be they positive or negative, in order to empower their journey. My deepest hope is that this book will continue that journey of learning and empowerment for scholars and practitioners involved in global work.

Research Design, Methodology Details, and Sample

My work has sought to fill theoretical and empirical gaps that can have a profound impact on global work. I conducted many in-depth studies focused on the intrapersonal, interpersonal, and intergroup challenges people encountered in global communication and investigated how language challenges influenced the ways in which workers—particularly non-native speakers—experienced themselves, their collaboration partners (other foreign non-native speakers as well as native speakers), and their organizations. I began to publish papers and present at conferences, introducing the subject of lingua franca and its dilemmas for global work to the organizational studies field.[1]

One of the logical next steps for my work was a longitudinal research study that would capture the evolution of a lingua franca in a single company over an extended period of time. Because language issues are inextricably linked to globalization I wanted to capture processes and outcomes in a company that had an expressed interest in global expansion and its attendant cultural exchanges. To truly understand the role a lingua franca transformation could play in an organization's globalization agenda, I needed to design and conduct a study that was longitudinal, gather data from multiple members across multiple country sites, and use a hybrid approach to analyze qualitative and quantitative data. Rakuten's Englishnization mandate provided an ideal setting to fulfill all those research design goals. I was fortunate to begin studying Rakuten's journey to lingua franca from almost the beginning.

Data Sources

Over a period of five years, my approach resulted in the sample study, which informs this book, and is comprised of 650 interviews across 8 country sites in 5 languages, a total of 3,056 quantitative survey data collected twice (1,564 respondents in the first round and 1,492 respondents six months later), including 660 open-ended optional comments responses, 183 open-ended responses, and over 20,000 pages of archival data (see Table A.1 for more information about the data sources for this book).

TABLE A.1. Interview Summary

Location	Membership	Native Language	Age Range in Years	Informants' Gender	Number of Interviews
Brazil	Acquired 2011	Portuguese	24–48	62% Male 38% Female	29
France	Acquired 2010	French	21–41	65% Male 35% Female	85
Germany	Acquired 2011	German	21–47	71% Male 29% Female	28
Indonesia	Acquired 2011	Indonesian	22–45	58% Male 42% Female	25
Japan	Founded 1997	Japanese	22–55	75% Male 25% Female	306
Taiwan	Acquired 2008	Mandarin	24–46	30% Male 70% Female	16
Thailand	Acquired 2009	Thai	27–48	54% Male 46% Female	21
United States (three entities)	Acquired 2005, 2009, 2010	English	21–62	64% Male 36% Female	140
				Total Interviews = 650	

Surveys			
Japan	Wave 1—May 2011		1,564
Japan	Wave 2—November 2011		1,492
		Total Surveys = 3,056	

Archival Documents	> 20,000 pages
Optional Narratives	660
Open-Ended Surveys	183

Note: Twenty translators in five languages participated in this study.

FIELD INTERVIEW DATA

I rigorously trained a team of 13 bilingual researchers in qualitative data collection techniques, who also traveled to various country sites to gather data for this study, We conducted semi-structured interviews with the 650 members of Rakuten located across 8 country sites, including Brazil, France, Germany, Indonesia, Japan (headquarters), Taiwan, Thailand, and three locations in the United States. The country sites that I selected, from a list of countries in which Rakuten operated, represented important markets for the company's global strategy. I chose semi-structured interviews, an approach that includes a set of prepared questions, yet is open to covering areas that are most pressing or salient to the interviewees, because it allowed us to expand into unexplored territory, seek alternative accounts on a given topic, or adapt our interview questions and construct new lines of questioning on the fly.

Prior to my arrival or my research team members' arrival to the various country sites, the subsidiary leaders sent out e-mails inviting employees to participate in a study about their experience of the English language mandate at Rakuten. Participants were assured that interviews would be both voluntary and anonymous. In most cases, we limited our informants to those who had tenure at Rakuten for at least one year prior to the announcement of the lingua franca mandate. This ensured that informants could discuss their organizational life before and after the language stipulation. In certain circumstances, a country site was acquired post-adoption of the lingua franca, rendering the tenure requirement inapplicable.

Interviews were conducted in person with a few exceptions when scheduling issues dictated they be conducted by telephone. Interviews lasted 45 to 75 minutes and were held in either private offices or conference rooms. Informants were interviewed according to their individual language preferences. Overall, 53 interviews were conducted in French, 20 in German, 29 in Portuguese, and 128 in Japanese; the remaining interviews were conducted in English. Table A.1 summarizes the number of informant interviews we conducted in each country site and includes demographic information on age and gender. Forty informants were interviewed twice, 15 were interviewed a third time, and 8 were interviewed 7 times in order to track changes people were experiencing over time as a result of the English language mandate. Each interview was recorded on a digital audio recorder with the informant's permission.

Interview protocols were primarily organized into four sections, in line with standard procedures for conducting semi-structured interviews.[2] The first section covered background questions, including work history at the organization, demographic details, and a description of current job roles. We made sure to capture a baseline of information for each interviewee.

In the second section, we focused on questions pertaining to informants' perspectives and experiences. We asked informants to provide in-depth descriptions about their daily tasks and how language affected those tasks, if at all. Sample prompts in the section included: "What role has the language mandate played in your daily work?" and "What do you think of the policy? Is it right for the organization?" In the third section, we investigated how the language affected informants' daily interactions both within and between country locations; for example, we asked: "In your work, with whom do you interact most often?" "In what ways do you communicate within and across company locations?" "How has Englishnization changed your work?" In the fourth section, we posed grand tour questions; for example: "Describe your typical work week." This allowed us to follow up with mini-tour questions that could uncover details about specific events and participants.[3] We found this line of inquiry useful in probing delicate subjects such as perceived changes associated with the introduction of the lingua franca, how the informants' feelings might have evolved relative to the mandate, or informants' impressions of the mandate's potential impact.

Given the large scope and scale of the research design, with 13 interviewers collecting data from over 650 people across 8 countries, I developed rules to ensure thorough and consistent documentation. During the data collection phase, each researcher generated three forms of field notes, which I had adapted from Yin.[4] The first form captured demographic data within a standard template, noted the most salient points that surfaced during each interview, listed informants' discussions of post–lingua franca work practices, and described interactions between country sites and headquarters. The second form, a comprehensive memo written at the conclusion of each researcher's data-gathering day, chronicled the thoughts and ideas that flowed following a collection of interviews. Finally, the third form consisted of a single case summary created by each researcher upon completion at a given country site. For example, if five researchers conducted interviews in France, they would each generate a case summary, yielding five summaries for that location. The case summary reflected a synthesis of daily memos and emergent themes, primarily on how the change to a lingua franca impacted informants' organizational lives. I read the field notes shortly after they were generated to remain adaptive and alert to emerging patterns, insights, and concepts.[5] Importantly, the three forms of field notes set the foundation for both individual and cross-case analyses that I discuss later.

All interviews were transcribed verbatim, and those conducted in a language other than English were translated into English. I took several steps to ensure that the translated interviews were identical to the original language version. First, I recruited translators who specialized in translating the specific language (e.g., Portuguese, German, or French) to English. Second, additional translators blind to the original interview performed a back translation on a random selection of these transcripts. If there were discrepancies between the original and the back translated material, additional translators were recruited to translate the transcripts anew until the original language version and the translation were equivalent. (Note: In total, twenty translators participated in this research study.)

Occasionally my research team and I sat in on meetings at the various country locations. For example, in Thailand, we observed the Asakai company-wide meeting where CEO Mikitani gave a presentation via videoconference from the headquarters in Tokyo. We attended Asakia meetings in France, Germany, and Taiwan, providing us with cases for comparison. Attending group events helped us gain a richer understanding of informants' experiences and vantage points, as well as the overall organizational context.

FIELD INTERVIEW ANALYSIS

Following Strauss and Corbin's[6] recommended practices for qualitative analysis, we began by aggregating interview transcripts by country locations into NVivo qualitative research software. While in the field, I had sensed differences between narratives from the various groups within the company but did not have a systematic grasp on how those differences played out. To develop a theoretical account of how the mandate affected employees given their specific cultural and linguistic backgrounds, my research team and I spent two years painstakingly coding the data through several iterative stages.

The first stage entailed open coding, in which we associated the data with codes (categorized labels). Non-native English speakers from the Tokyo headquarters (mostly Japanese) had to adapt linguistically to comply with the English mandate, while native English speakers, impacted by the increased interaction between offices as a result of the mandate, were obliged to adapt culturally. This led me to label the non-native speakers based in the Japanese office as "linguistic expats" and the U.S.-based employees as "cultural expats." In addition, the non-native speakers in the various subsidiaries (Brazil, France, Germany, Taiwan, Thailand, and Indonesia) who were not part of the Japanese country headquarters had to adapt linguistically *and* culturally. I labeled that group the "linguistic-cultural expats."

In the course of our analysis, we cycled back and forth between data analysis and the literature to make sense of emerging concepts and to refine our codes. Similar to the interview process, our team wrote memos to capture our reflections following each coding session. This activity served as a foundation to ground the research and eased the transition from coding data to conceptualizing.[7] Again, I read every memo on the day it was produced so that I could remain alert to any emerging concepts that may have required adapting codes across the board.

During the second stage of coding we began axial coding, which entailed categorizing and organizing codes by evaluating their corresponding relationships. While coding for any given group (the point at which I began to think of three archetypical social groups), we first queried the data for employees' experience of and response to the linguistic and cultural shifts taking place within the organization. These experiences and responses were multifaceted and led to an iterative process of creating, reevaluating, refining, and abandoning codes. For example, cultural expats' positive responses toward the mandate were emblematic, at least initially, of euphoria. As we went deeper into the data, it became apparent that this euphoria was connected to the anticipation of future benefits, or as a direct experience of positive benefits. Specific benefits evidenced in the codes included "enhanced communication" and "increased knowledge sharing."

In a similar way, cultural shifts were documented in the coding process based on cultural expats' experience of the cultural infusion from headquarters. For example, we created codes for the weekly company-wide meetings Rakuten held within each subsidiary. Similarly, codes were created for headquarters-hosted conferences, which involved subsidiary members traveling to Tokyo to attend trainings, conferences, and other events. As informants referred to more such practices, it became clear that "work practices," defined as the ways of accomplishing work within the organization, was a high-level category, capturing one way that Japanese culture infused the company culture. Alongside "work practices" were other high-level categories: "values," defined as the organization's guiding principles that direct employee behavior, and "artifacts," items that are culturally significant and convey information from headquarters, such as posters and publications.

Subsequently, we began the cross-case analysis stage[8] by looking for patterns manifesting laterally across country sites (country ↔ country) and vertically between country sites and headquarters (country ↔ headquarters). Iteratively, we performed the data analysis, hypothesized relevant constructs, assessed these constructs and any inconsistencies present, revisited the data, and then decided whether the construct should be abandoned or refined.

As we continued to code and analyze, it became apparent that each archetype contained adaptive and less adaptive "expats" with respect to their global work experience. We looked again at the linguistic-cultural expats, the group who had most successfully adapted to the new organizational environment brought about by the lingua franca mandate. As we investigated these dual expats' attitudes and behaviors, we noted in our provisional codes a pattern of an open disposition to working across national borders, a category we labeled "global work orientation."

Two research assistants and I coded the data separately in order to identify the dimensions that comprised the concept of global work orientation. We met frequently to discuss the codes and to ensure that we could capture the nuances of the concept. We iterated multiple conceptual models as we sought to understand how potential codes might interact or otherwise work in concert. In this same vein, we iteratively analyzed our models against the data to test our emergent theory of global work orientation, and referenced related literature when applicable to sharpen our conceptualization. For example, we created a provisional code for "thinking globally" when our interviewees expressed the virtues of a global mind-set. Yet upon review, the codes that we developed to capture patterns on thinking globally were not sufficiently consistent with our definition of thinking globally; nor were they pervasive enough. We ultimately rejected this aspect of the model.

The final model that inductively and robustly captured the concept of global work orientation had five elements. The first captured the manner in which the dual expats' narrative projected a benevolent attitude, coupled with expressions that diminished the heaviness of having to adopt certain foreign cross-cultural practices (e.g., Adopting this custom is not that serious; I'll try it). We labeled this element "positive indifference." Second, analysis uncovered a pattern in which the dual expats espoused a willingness to find commonality between cultures in statements about foreign colleagues as well as in response to the influx of Japanese cultural values that came from Rakuten's headquarters (e.g., Our culture has similar customs). Third, our analysis surfaced sentiments that encompassed dual

"Got it!" Digger said.

He hopped into the car.

Dadasaur drove into town.

He turned left.

Then he turned right.

"I don't see a cake shop,"
said Dadasaur.
"Can you call Mom?"

Digger dialed Momasaur's
number.
"Hello? Hello?"
Digger asked.
"Did we pass what?"

"Did you pass a park?"
Momasaur asked.

"A shark!?" yelled Digger.

"PARK," said Momasaur.

"Oh!" said Digger.

"Park! Yes we did."

"Do you see the blue house?"
Momasaur asked.

"STOP!" said Digger.

Dadasaur stopped the car.
Digger and Dad got out.
"The new house!"
said Digger.

"No, Digger,"
said Momasaur.
"BLUE, not new."
"Got it," said Digger.

"I still don't see
a cake shop,"
said Dadasaur.

"I know!" said Digger.
"I ride bikes here with Stego.
We saw a cake shop."

Digger pointed to the right.
"Then we need to brake,"
said Dadasaur.

"We need a CAKE,"
said Digger.
Dadasaur roared.

"Good thing you came with me," said Dadasaur. "Very good thing," said Digger.

Digger went into the shop.

He came back with a big cake.

"Next stop, home!" he said.

"We take a right here,"
said Dadasaur.
"A BITE here?!"
asked Digger.

"Don't you dare,"
said Dadasaur.
"Got it," said Digger.

Foreword

1O SIMPLE THINGS YOU CAN DO TO IMPROVE YOUR MEMORY (The Memory Manual) is an informative, upbeat, and positive approach toward resolving the difficulties people experience with their own memory lapses or with those of a loved one.

This book will be treasured by those who are looking for practical ways to improve memory. They will appreciate the vignettes that make the theory come alive, the exercises for personal application, and the chapter themes that illustrate continuing concerns.

It is comprehensive. Few books related to memory have the breadth and depth of research that this one has in support of its findings and guidance. With each chapter, the author's focus on information, applications, and steps to take to improve one's memory is useful and refreshing.

The subject is very timely. As people are living longer today than in previous generations, they are concerned about what they tend to forget in the present, what they forget from the past, and what they may forget in the future.

10 Simple Things You Can Do to Improve Your Memory is a beacon to thoughtful men and women who are seeking a solid foundation to understand how memory works and what to do to improve it. Educators and health care professionals should recommend it to their students and clients, and individuals should recommend it to family and friends.

I hope you read it, learn from it, and enjoy the process.

—MURIEL JAMES, author/coauthor of *Passion for Life: Psychology and the Human Spirit, Born to Win: Transactional Analysis with Gestalt Experiments, It's Never Too Late to be Happy* and 16 other books.

Acknowledgments

I AM TAKING THIS OPPORTUNITY to express my deep gratitude to a number of people who have influenced and inspired my thinking.

I am indebted to Gertrude Hall who recruited me to direct the Tri-City Project on Aging. Her enthusiasm about a satisfying life style for older people continues to be contagious.

I am indebted to the faculty and participants in the summer institutes in the 1970s at the Andrus Gerontology Center of the University of Southern California. They brought a wealth of experiences from their varied disciplines to create a fantastic learning environment the memory of which continues to inspire me after over twenty-five years. I felt particularly indebted to James Birren, Ruth Weg, Vern Bengtson, Allan Knox and to Gloria Haerther Cavanaugh who kept it all running smoothly year after year.

During the intervening years, my teaching and writing in gerontology and how to improve the quality of life in retirement have benefitted greatly from the writings and insights of specialists in the field of aging too numerous to mention.

Other areas of research have also made significant contributions to the program in *10 Simple Things You Can Do To Improve Your Memory*. Marian Diamond has discovered the importance of a rich environment for memory functioning. Robert Sapolsky's research has revealed the physical impact of stress on memory and ways to compensate.

I am indebted to Muriel James, my mentor and friend, who has developed creative ways for people to make the changes enabling them to take charge of their lives.

I am indebted to Viktor Frankl for his writing on the search for meaning, which is critical to memory, and to Martin Buber for his concept of the life of dialogue, which opens people to the transcendent experiences which are intensely memorable.

I am indebted to the hundreds of my students who have shared their lives and cooperated in the process of creating a memory program which really works for people over the long term and regardless of age. Many students have given me valuable feedback and have agreed to my telling their stories provided their privacy was protected. These anecdotes have made the program come alive for people who have read the manuscript for this book.

I am indebted to John James and the members of his Writers' Workshop, particularly Eugene Merlin, Sue Hughes, and Ibis Schlesinger-James, who have been constantly supportive in giving me straight feedback and encouragement with this book during its long and difficult gestation.

I have appreciated Danielle Lapp's sharing with me her experiences in teaching memory strategies to older adults.

I am indebted to my children Betsy and Fred, who have critiqued the manuscript. From their different perspectives, they have identified what worked for them in this memory program. I am deeply grateful for their help and encouragement.

And, finally, I am indebted to my publisher Steve Mettee and Marsh Cassady for editing this book. *10 Simple Things You Can Do To Improve Your Memory* has gained a great deal from their skills and commitment to its success and I am most appreciative.

Introduction

Do you forget appointments?
Have you ever arrived promptly on the wrong day?

Do you have trouble remembering names or faces?

Do you often forget where you put your car keys? As a matter of fact, have you ever mislaid your car?

Everyone has occasional memory problems because of the multitude of demands on our attention, and everyone has a gap between actual and potential memory ability. *10 Simple Things You Can Do To Improve Your Memory: The Memory Manual* is a simple, holistic program you can use to tap into your own natural resources to span that gap. Your rewards will be to increase your memory skills and to improve the quality of your life.

This is a program I have used in numerous memory training classes I have conducted in the course of my twenty-five years of study and teaching in the field of aging. Many success stories have emerged from these training classes.

> "For twenty years I've been raising a family," Mary Johnson remarked after one such class. "Now I'm doing something just for me. I've always wanted to go to college, but lately I've been worried that my memory wouldn't be up to it.
>
> "I almost let that worry keep me from going back to school. But I've learned here how to help myself remember better, and now I'm confident I'll do fine in college."

Henry Davis mailed his evaluation:

"I was sorry to miss the last class but we were on a cruise. There were ten people at our table, and I knew all their names by dinner the second night. And, what's more, I still remember them! One of my reasons for taking your course was that I just couldn't remember names."

Marcia Douglas wrote:

"The class has helped me learn how my feelings affect my memory. This has been a hard year for me with my husband's death and worries about the kids. Here I've learned how I can slow down to focus on one thing at a time and take some control of the stresses in my life. The bonus is that my memory has really improved."

It is my sincere hope that you too will experience some of the same success as you apply the principles in this book.

TEN STEPS TO A GOOD MEMORY

There are ten basic areas to concentrate on when working to improve your memory skills.

- Gain an understanding of how your memory works.
- Develop memory tools to assist you.
- Find the motivation and make a commitment.
- Enjoy life and continue to grow as a human being.
- Increase your ability to focus on what's at hand.
- Organize both how you learn and how you live.

- Take care of your health.
- Deal with stress and depression.
- Understand and cope with the natural aging process.
- Become your own mentor in support of your memory improvement program.

10 Simple Things You Can Do To Improve Your Memory focuses on reinforcing the natural memory process. You remember naturally when you are motivated to pay attention and to concentrate enough to integrate the specific items you want or need to remember.

Identify your goals for a better memory, then adopt the everyday habits and lifestyle patterns that will enable you to reach them.

ONE

Understand How Your Memory Works

WE REMEMBER SOME THINGS without difficulty—the birth of a child, a trip to Yosemite National Park, or the year the home team came from the bottom of the league to win the pennant.

Creating such memories happens naturally. The natural way to remember an event is to be caught up in it. When this happens, you think about it, compare it in your mind with other events, and, perhaps, discuss it with your friends. You may even decide to take some kind of action like making a donation or writing a poem. All of these factors work together to create a memory.

Yet everybody has memory lapses. We forget because we're human. Our many thoughts, feelings, needs, and desires are in frequent competition. Each of us lives in the midst of a buffet of choices, stimulations to the senses, and demands on our attention. Sometimes this attention is grabbed away from one pressing concern by another with a louder voice. This often creates a memory lapse.

Meeting an old friend unexpectedly during a trip to the grocery store may erase the most essential article from your mental shopping list. A telephone call while you're planning an agenda for a meeting may be so distracting that you forget to include a crucial committee report.

Thoughts and feelings also usurp attention. Mulling over whether or not to spend the money to repaint the house, you may leave home for the supermarket and suddenly find yourself on the way to the post office. Worry over an ongoing financial problem may cause you to misplace your keys or even to forget where you've put the car.

Like burglars in the night, such memory lapses may leave you feeling angry and perhaps worried about what they might mean for the future. However, with a little thought and a willingness to make a few modest lifestyle changes, you can ease your concerns and prevent these common, garden-variety memory lapses.

Taken together, the ten simple steps presented in this book comprise an effective program for improving your memory. The first phase of your program is to understand the memory process. You can then become more aware of your own memory at work and increase control over your ability to recall whatever has priority for you.

Unraveling the Mysteries of Memory

Memory is the ability to register, combine, and store information from each of your senses, thoughts, feelings, and actions for you to recall when you want or need it.

Memory also is the result of this process, as, for example, the memory of a visit with an old friend.

THE PHYSICAL BASIS OF MEMORY

How the brain creates a memory has long been the subject of speculation and study, but doing research on the living human brain presents obvious difficulties. Laboratory studies of other nonhuman forms of life such as apes, rats, and jellyfish, however, have provided many insights. Additionally, as a result of accidents or when lifesaving surgery is needed, doctors have learned what happens when parts of the brain are damaged or removed. Further, modern technology has provided noninvasive ways of viewing the brain at work. As a result, more of the mystery is being solved.

What we do understand about the physical basis of memory helps provide a frame of reference for its improvement. Memory is a function of your brain and nervous system, which consist of many billions of nerve cells or neurons. In this electrochemical system the neurons are the wiring.

A neuron is composed of a cell body with two kinds of extensions: numerous dendrites and, usually, a single axon. Dendrites are hairlike branchings from the cell which collect information. The axon is a long and thicker arm which acts as a transmitter in passing information along to another neuron in the brain.

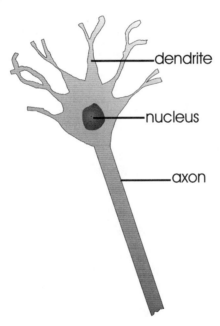

A neuron, shown here highly magnified, consists of the cell body, branching dendrites, and an axon.

The point of contact between two neurons is the synapse, a kind of docking place on a dendrite where new data is accepted from another cell's axon. A dendrite may have several of these docking places. At the synapse, the axon releases a chemical, a neurotransmitter, which enables information to cross the tiny gap between the two neurons.

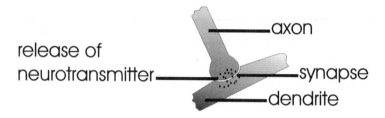

At the synapse, the axon releases a neurotransmitter which enables the dendrite to receive information in the form of an electrical impulse. (Shown highly magnified.)

Each neuron has a specialty. Some handle information from the senses. Others deal with thoughts, feelings, and actions. Distinct areas of the brain, called brain centers, process information for each of these special functions. Each bit of data collected by a dendrite is converted into an electrical impulse which travels through the cell and along the axon to the next cell until it reaches the appropriate neuron in the appropriate brain center.

A neuron functions by firing (like a gun), so it can carry only one kind of information (a bullet). Therefore, when you look at a pink rose, different visual neurons sense the color pink, the shape of the flower, and its position on the stem. When you feel the rose, different tactile neurons sense the velvet of a petal, the woody texture of the stem, and the prickle of a thorn.

As the data collected by neurons are sent to brain centers, they become memory traces. This information from the senses, along with your thoughts, feelings, and actions, is consolidated in the brain. This involves putting together the bits of current information and then relating the information to memories from the past and expectations for the future.

For example, when eating a chocolate chip cookie, you can experience it with each of your senses. Since a neuron carries just one unique bit of information, all the specific qualities registered by each of the senses will be handled by different neurons:

- vision neurons will register the cookie's color, size, shape, and context
- taste neurons—sweetness
- smell neurons—brown sugar, chocolate
- touch neurons—smoothness, lumpiness
- hearing neurons—crunch
- movement neurons—crispness, chewy quality

As you eat the cookie, each of these twelve elements becomes a sensory memory trace.

Your brain centers dealing with thought also register data on this cookie. You can compare it with others in texture and flavor. You might recall that the first chocolate chip cookies were named for the Toll House on Cape Cod. You remember having lunch there many years ago. You may also anticipate your granddaughter's visit tomorrow when she will make chocolate chip cookies. The result of all this is called thought traces, which are a specific sort of memory trace.

At the same time these other things are occurring, you may act by walking into your kitchen and checking the cupboard to be sure the ingredients are on hand for tomorrow. Through actions you create motor traces, another type of memory trace.

You may feel nostalgia for the past, enjoyment of this cookie, and happiness at the thought of spending some time with your granddaughter. These are feeling traces.

Remarkably, the connections among your brain centers are so organized that any of these memory traces can recall for you the experience of eating this chocolate chip cookie.

The more you sense, think, feel, and take action with regard to any item or event, the more memory traces you create and the more memorable this item or event will be.

THE PHYSICAL BASIS FOR A BETTER MEMORY

The numbers of dendrites and synapses, with their supply of neurotransmitters, seem to determine the amount of information which you can learn and remember. Research has demonstrated that dendrites and synapses grow in size and number relative to how stimulating one's environment is. This is true regardless of age. In *Enriching Heredity: The Impact of the Environment on the Anatomy of the Brain*, Marian Cleeves Diamond discusses what happened with rats placed in three types of environments:

- an "impoverished" environment where rats were placed alone in small cages;
- a "standard" environment with three rats to a cage, and
- an "enriched" environment in which twelve rats were placed in a large cage where they had lots of contact with each other.

Each day rats in the enriched environment were given two of seven different toys, and each day for thirty minutes they could explore a maze with movable sections representing different levels of problem solving. Sugar pellets were given as rewards.

These rats showed an increase in the diameter of blood vessels supplying nutrition to the brain. Brain weight also significantly increased—seventy-five percent in the visual area and sixty-four percent in other areas. The increased size of the brain reflected an increase in the size of brain cells, not an increase in the number of cells. With the increased blood flow, brain cells were better fed and grew more dendrites and synapses.

Rats in the other cages did not show an increase in brain weight. Simply being with a couple of other rats was not stimulating enough to increase brain capacity. Brain growth required interaction with the other rats and response to the challenges represented by the toys and mazes.

This research suggests couch potatoes may not receive the stimulation necessary to grow new dendrites and increase the number of synapses. For this to happen, you need to seek out environments or situations that allow you to interact with others and to learn new things. Doing this will improve your nerve functioning and allow you to learn more easily, live a fuller and a richer life, and at the same time improve your memory.

Although research has provided much information about how memory works, the most tantalizing mystery remains: How does your brain consolidate all this information? The incredible complexity of this system is astounding. On demand, your memory can supply you with:

- a view of the Parthenon under a full moon, the awe you felt at such beauty, and your thoughts about how it must have looked in the classical age of Greece with its roof intact and the sculptured figures in place

- the tiny face of a new baby and your joy at the miracle of his birth
- the value for Pi, 3.1416
- the first two lines of the national anthem

Your memory will not confuse Einstein's equation, $E = mc2$ with *pi* or the French *La Marseillaise* with *The Star Spangled Banner*. You will not be reminded of your great aunt's Victorian house instead of the Parthenon, or Baby Face Nelson instead of a newborn baby.

These examples illustrate the two ways of acquiring a memory. The first two are instances of incidental learning, which happens in the process of living. These are the people, places, things, events, and ideas that catch your attention. The last two reflect intentional learning, the sort that takes place when you are committed to mastering new information.

INCIDENTAL LEARNING

Incidental learning occurs as you become aware of and respond to the experiences of your life. It may occur when you see your first play by Shakespeare and marvel not only at his poetic and dramatic skill but at a cast's fine performance. It may take place at a Little League baseball game as you watch a young relative hit his first home run.

You remember births, graduations and weddings because they have special meaning and because you review them often, in your mind or in talking with others. Special memories may include personal achievements, positive experiences of beauty, precious moments shared with loved ones, or events imbued with the joy of living.

Other incidental happenings filled with meaning and thus well remembered may be the death of a loved one, the loss of a treasure you cannot replace, or suffering which you are unable to avoid.

New experiences can change the way incidental memories are recalled. The following demonstrates how this happens.

> David Arnold heard Wagner's *Der Ring des Niebelungen* performed only once—at the Metropolitan Opera House in New York. He often enjoyed remembering that magnificent music in the impressive atmosphere of the Met.
>
> In touring Germany a few years later, David saw the gigantic cave near Linderhof castle where the demented King Ludwig arranged for the *Ring* to be performed for his pleasure.
>
> Now when David hears any of the *Ring* music he imagines mad King Ludwig in all his finery listening to that powerful music alone in the starkness of his cave.

David's experience is an example of how a later, related event can provide a new context within which to view the original experience.

INTENTIONAL LEARNING

Intentional learning involves acquiring new information—new memory traces—by deliberately seeking, creating, and reviewing new connections with what you already know. For instance, if you are studying Spanish and find the word *sala* means room you might make a connection with the English word *salon*, also a room. For the word *sala* you would have the following memory traces:

- the visual trace from reading *sala*
- the motor trace from saying *sala* aloud
- the auditory trace from hearing yourself say it
- the thought trace from connecting *sala* with *salon*

The thought trace would reinforce the sensory and motor traces. Review along with using the word in sentences would rapidly make the word well-stored and part of your active vocabulary.

Often incidental and intentional learning are related.

Martha Brewer had been a widow for fifteen years when her brother-in-law died and she received a family Bible. It contained vital records and clippings about events in the lives of the Conaway and Butterfield families in Portland, Kentucky.

"How interesting! Martha thought. She'd not previously heard of these people and never knew her husband was related to a Methodist minister from Kentucky.

She was touched by the pressed flowers and loving greeting cards hidden away in the Bible and decided to make a project out of putting together a family history for her children.

Martha took courses in genealogy and learned how to research census, county, city, and church records.

Incidental learning acquired from a family Bible motivated Martha toward intentional learning about how to explore the many avenues of genealogical research.

*   *   *

The focus of this book is on improving both incidental and intentional memory. As you become more open to and aware of other people, places, and events, you'll incidentally become more sensitive to the unique qualities which make everyday experiences easy to remember.

A brilliant sunset, an unexpected letter from an old friend, an insight which solves a problem, or a deer on the lawn can become a vignette which is meaningful and memorable.

In contrast, intentional learning results from curiosity and the motivation to commit your time and energy to learning something you find significant, as Martha decided to do with her husband's family tree. Both types of learning are stored in your memory bank through a three-stage process.

Stages of Memory

Memory occurs in three stages:

- *sensory* memory
- *short term* memory with *working* memory
- *long term* memory

Sensory and short term memory are temporary activities of your conscious mind, which has a limited capacity. Long term memory is not conscious and virtually unlimited. It consists of material that has been filed away and which you can bring back into consciousness.

Research indicates that sensory and short term memory are maintained by repetitive electrical impulses. Long term memory, however, seems to be a biochemical change involving what happens between neurons at the synapse.

As we progress through this book, you will discover that you can take increasing control of your memory at any stage.

SENSORY MEMORY
Sensory memory lasts a few seconds or less, just long enough to respond to something you sense. For instance, this immediate memory enables a typist to operate a typewriter or computer. As each

word is typed, the sensory memory of it disappears. Thus no word interferes with the one that follows it.

Here is another example:

> Barbara Carter is driving down the freeway, with cars of different colors whizzing by in the left lane. Each of these cars is a sensory memory which immediately will disappear from her awareness unless it catches her attention. Barbara, however, is engrossed in thinking about a three o'clock meeting with her lawyer Henry Wilson.
>
> That evening she is getting dinner while her husband is listening to the news in the den. Suddenly he calls to her, "Hey, honey, did you hear about a robbery this afternoon?"
>
> "No, why?"
>
> "It was at that gas station across from Henry's. News report said it was about three this afternoon. A man driving a green station wagon."
>
> "I was there," Barbara answered, "But I didn't see any green station wagon."

That afternoon Barbara's thoughts about the approaching appointment were too absorbing for her to notice anything other than her driving.

However, a sensory memory which attracts your attention does not disappear. Instead, the sensation enters short term memory, where it stays as long as you continue to pay attention to it.

Here's a different scenario:

> Molly Drum, on a shopping trip, is driving down the freeway, with cars of different colors whizzing by in the left lane. Each is

a sensory memory which will disappear from her awareness unless it catches her attention. Suddenly one of them does, a cherry-red convertible. Molly swings her slate gray station wagon in behind the red car. Wow—what a beauty! she thinks.

The red car had caught Molly's attention and moved from her sensory to short term memory.

SHORT TERM MEMORY

Short term memory is also a temporary memory. Here new information is both stored and sorted before it is recorded permanently or lost through lack of attention.

Memory lapses often occur because the capacity of short term memory is limited to five to seven items. However, items are held as long as you continue to give them your attention.

Working memory is the term used for the processing of information you are holding in short term memory. This may include sensory data, feelings, thoughts, or plans for action. In this stage, you can sort, compare, and connect new information either with other new data or that which was previously stored in your long term memory. Typically, it is this processing of thoughts and feelings which moves experiences into your long term memory.

To continue the example of Molly and the convertible:

Molly kept thinking about the red car. She thought of the first car she and her husband had owned. It was a red convertible, too. A real joy, but it finally got too expensive to repair. Since then, they'd driven practical family cars. Now, she thought, with the kids all grown, it was time for something jazzy. What she really wanted was another red convertible!

If she got a job, she could pay for it herself. She didn't think Paul would mind and, with the kids gone, she had a lot of free time.

I'll talk to him tonight, she told herself. Then if it's OK, she'd call her former boss tomorrow. He always said to let him know if she ever wanted to come back to work.

In this example, Molly kept the red car in mind by:

- thinking of her feelings about this color and model of car and of a new car
- planning to pay for it by getting a job
- deciding to discuss her plan with Paul and, if he agreed, to contact her former boss

This processing insured that the red convertible and related thoughts and feelings would be stored in Molly's long term memory.

Molly may have gone on imagining how her life would be different if she had a new car. Or she may have figured out how long it would take to pay for a car like that if she got a job. Collecting new information, thinking about it, talking about it, and any other related action would insure that the information was retained and further integrated into Molly's long term memory.

LONG TERM MEMORY

Long term memory, that is, your memory bank, has an estimated capacity of hundreds of times the contents of the Encyclopaedia Britannica. For practical purposes, the storage space is unlimited.

Information in long term memory seems to be stored through new and changing connections between neurons at the synapses. Although memory traces from your senses, thoughts, feelings, and actions are stored in different centers in the brain, these traces are so interconnected that any one or several of them may recall a complete event.

Some people find smells to be particularly evocative reminders. For instance, if you grew up in New England, just the smell of frying clams may bring back memories of family rides on summer afternoons with the usual stop for Johnson's fried clams. You may, in your mind's eye, see your father returning to the car with the white cardboard cartons filled to the brim with fragrant brown clams.

As we discussed, recall is easier when there is a variety of memory traces.

> Doug Evans attended his thirty-fifth high school reunion. It was the first time he had been back since graduation. A man who looked familiar came up to greet him, but Doug couldn't remember his name.
>
> The man said, "Surely you remember me. We used to play tennis on Friday afternoons."
>
> Then Doug knew immediately who he was and said, "Of course I do. You're John Nelson. Maybe we could get in some tennis while I'm here. You used to live on Elm Street. And, say, whatever became of your sister Judy? She was a beauty."

Although the cue of a familiar face did not produce a name, the cue of Friday afternoon tennis brought back not only John's name but other information about him as well. If the two men continued reminiscing, they might have found other old memories emerging like links in a chain.

Freshly acquired long term memory may be less stable than older long term memory since the latter may have been reinforced by recall and review over time. A year from now Molly's memory of the red car may be vivid depending on ensuing events. If she does, in fact, get a job and buy a red convertible this experience may become part of the history of her new car. Occasional recall and retelling over the years will establish the memory securely.

If, however, that same day Molly's husband is assigned to a new job in London, the incident of the red convertible may fade. Some years later, when Molly sees a red convertible, she may not remember this incident. On the other hand, she may recall having thought about a red convertible on the very day Paul was transferred to London.

In summary, these three stages of memory have a linear relationship. When a sensory memory draws attention, it enters short term memory where working memory processes the new data for integration into long term memory.

The stages are also interdependent. Sensory and short term memory provide new information to update long term memory, which is the database used by working memory to process new material in short term memory.

Contents of Memory

Memory holds two kinds of material:

- *knowledge* which can be consciously recalled or recognized
- mental or physical *procedures* performed without the need for conscious awareness of the process

KNOWLEDGE
Knowledge is of two types: general and personal.

General knowledge is accumulated through formal and informal education and the experience of living. This includes the style and patterns of your culture. You can continue adding to this storehouse throughout your life. These memories do not change except as you alter or add to them with new data. They may, however, become faint with disuse or if they are not well learned initially.

Personal knowledge, on the other hand, refers to the events and experiences of your own life. These memories may change significantly over time. The reason is that when a memory is recalled, it is affected by your situation, thoughts, and feelings at the time you are recalling it.

For instance, the loss of a $5 bill could seem tragic if you've just lost your job. However, if you find a new job with a large raise, your recall of the loss may become less emotional. In time, the memory may fade completely, only to be recalled if someone reminds you of it.

Other changes in memories of past events may result from personal growth which changes perspectives. Anger and rebellion against a parent or authority figure may change radically when you yourself become the parent or authority figure. As a result, old related memories can change or soften as well.

In addition, interference with one memory by another may take place where two events are very similar.

Charles Freeman and his brother Arthur were recalling family Christmas celebrations over the years. Arthur chuckled. "I like to remember our first Christmas in Philadelphia. That was the year Dad fell into the Christmas tree trying to put the star on top. Remember?"

"I remember his falling into the Christmas tree," Charles answered, "but that was the Christmas we spent in Washington. You must remember, we were having that big party. We had to turn the tree around to hide the broken branch."

"You're wrong! I don't remember a thing about having a big party in Washington. Sometimes I think we didn't even grow up in the same family!"

Each person does remember differently. No doubt, if we listened longer to Charles and Arthur they would come to some agreement as to the place where Dad fell into the tree. Perhaps he did it both times, and the year of the big party was when Arthur was visiting a friend in New York.

When two people experience an event differently, their memories of it differ. This difference is compounded when, as each recalls the event, their individual memory of it is colored by the current situation and their feelings about it. In this way, memories of shared experiences often differ more with each passing year.

Sisters Dorothy and Mary Alice Gray shared their first roller coaster ride. Dorothy was a little scared, but she loved the sensation of soaring and then dropping down the curving track.

Mary Alice was so tense with fear she could not open her eyes. She gripped the hand rail so tightly that she had trouble moving her hands when the car stopped.

As we might expect, the sisters' memories of that ride differed. Every time either recalls the ride, her memory is affected by her more recent experiences.

Dorothy continued riding roller coasters from time to time and recalled that first event as a little tame by comparison with some later ones. Mary Alice vowed never to ride one again. She still recalls her one ride as traumatic.

PROCEDURES

A physical or mental procedure demands close attention while you are learning it. Once you have mastered the procedure, however, you don't have to think about it in order to do it. You can drive your car or ride your bicycle without having to pay attention to the process of starting, operating, and stopping it. Now you are free to focus on the route you are taking and assure yourself a safe ride.

A skilled typist does not have to pay attention either to the location or the act of typing each letter or syllable. He concentrates on the format and content.

Mental skills in procedural memory may include arithmetic or grammar and may consist of balancing an equation or diagramming a sentence.

Of course you may recall the day you received help from a tennis pro with your serve or the patience of a teacher coaching you on French pronunciation. But you will not have to remember the process of learning these skills in order to use them.

Complex skills that have gone unused for a long period often take extra time and attention to recall. You may have been a whiz at algebra years ago, but working with a quadratic equation today could require extra thinking. Such a skill, once recalled, will quickly become routine again. It merely had faded a little from disuse.

Memory for skills and procedures is not within the province of this book. Rather, the emphasis in this work is on improving your memory for general information and life experiences.

Exercises:
Identify Goals for Your Memory Project

1. Jot down on a sheet of paper any memory problems you experienced in the past week or two.
2. Can you identify any problems which may have been the result of passing thoughts having become lost from your short term memory before you had considered them enough to move them into your long term memory?
3. Keep a log of memory lapses as you go through this book. This will help you identify ways of preventing them and enhance your memory power. Include the date and time along with the memory lapse. Ask yourself, could I have prevented this? How?
4. What are your goals for improving your memory? Write them on a separate sheet of paper or on the first page of your log. Rate them according to your priorities with number one as the most important.

TWO

Equip Your
Memory Tool Chest

MEMORY TOOLS HELP YOU LEARN and store information for recall. There is nothing complicated or demanding about these tools; they are simply the natural abilities involved when you collect memory traces.

The next phase of your memory project is to become conscious of your own memory tools in action, to hone them a bit, and to decide to use them more often. Making this process an ongoing habit will improve your memory and enrich the quality of your everyday life.

Valuable memory tools are:

- sensory awareness
- mental images
- words and messages
- making associations and connections
- grouping
- repetition
- rehearsal and review
- spacing
- using memory aids as reminders

Tune In to Your Senses

Your basic five senses of sight, hearing, touch, taste, and smell, along with a kinesthetic sense from your body movement and an intuitive sense resulting from an inner perception of knowing, can supply a great deal of information in a short time.

The more you are conscious of what your senses are detecting, the more memory traces you collect, and the easier the experience will be to recall. For instance, when introduced to a stranger:

- Your eyes can observe the shade, style, and texture of hair; the color, shape, and expressions of eyes; unusual facial features; body size, shape, carriage and gestures, and style of clothing.
- Your ears can note the name and the qualities of the person's voice.
- Your nose can smell perfume, soap, shaving lotion, or other odors.
- Your touch and kinesthetic senses can feel the handshake. Is it tense or relaxed, cool or warm, firm or soft?
- Your intuition may tell you that the person is outgoing or reserved, energized or passive, enthusiastic or bored.

Sensory awareness of any moment is often the critical tool for recalling that moment.

- Seeing a fine color photograph of Lake Tahoe may bring back your first sight of the intense blue of the lake from Echo Summit and the awe you felt at that moment.

- A song at a concert may bring tears to your eyes as you recognize it as the same one your mother sang to you when you were a child. You feel again a little of the warmth of her tender care.

- The smell of an ocean breeze may cause you to recall the surge of excitement evoked by the first whiff of salt air when you were a youngster going to the beach.

- A tiny baby grasping your finger may remind you of another child reaching out to you.

- The spicy crunch of a bread and butter pickle may remind you of grandma in her white, bibbed apron canning pickles on the old wood stove at the farm, even though this occurred forty years ago and three thousand miles away.

People tend to vary in their reactions to sensory information. Some tend to notice visual sensations. Others respond more to the auditory aspects of an experience. For many people, the sense of smell is an unusually powerful reminder, and they can recognize individual people and places by their own unique odors. Ask yourself what types of sensory stimulation you respond to most readily.

Develop Mental Images

A mental image forms in your mind's eye when you recall a person, place, or thing which you have either actually seen or imagined. Such a mental picture is a useful memory tool because it is explicit, like a person's face, rather than abstract, like his name.

Mental images are personal and individual. If someone speaks of Katherine Hepburn, everyone present may remember her differently, perhaps as a young actress, a mature film star, or during her retirement years as she appeared in occasional interviews.

Forming a mental picture of a stranger as you are introduced, and recalling this image from time to time will help you recognize him in the future. This image also should include the context in which you met. In recalling a man you met in a clubhouse setting, you might think: I can see us standing in front of the fireplace and wondering where the manager got such fine big logs. Now what was his name? Oh, yes, it was Dave Perez.

Imagining a name tag on his lapel with "Dave Perez" written on it will create another memory trace to support the visual, auditory, and kinesthetic traces you collected during your conversation with him.

Creating mental pictures of fictitious people from an author's description will collect the extra traces that make these characters memorable and also enrich your experience of stories you read. Such images may be borrowed from real life, movies, or elsewhere. For instance, for a story about an old fisherman in his boat you might have a mental picture of Spencer Tracy in the final scenes of *The Old Man and the Sea* or an illustration in *Captain January*, a book you read as a child.

On the other hand, you may like to create completely new pictures based on information the author provides. These would probably be composites of people you have known or whose pictures you have seen. In either case, visualizing the characters' actions in each event makes the narrative more lively and memorable. It also is good practice for real-life events.

Mental images of places or things are valuable memory tools. Visualizing a map showing your way to an unfamiliar destination may create enough memory traces that you actually do not have to stop along the way to recheck the map. A habit of creating such mental images can keep you from getting lost and can speed your orientation to new localities.

If there is no road map available and you are relying on someone's verbal directions, convert the directions into a mental picture. In other words, visualize a map of the route to your destination. This creates another memory trace that makes you more apt to remember the directions.

Mental retracing creates a picture in which you imagine yourself reversing your path to find your way back to the place from which you started. This can help you locate an object you have misplaced.

You have an appointment, and you plan to cash a check on the way home. Checkbook in hand, you start for your car. The doorbell rings, and a delivery man asks you to sign for a package.

As you close the door, the dishwasher makes a clanking noise and you wonder, Should I call a repairman? Is it still under warranty? You decide to turn it off and check it when you get home.

You finally arrive at your car in a rush. You realize you're going to be late and you don't have your checkbook. Mental retracing, picturing yourself at the door and then at the dishwasher can quickly enable you to realize where you put it down.

You may often use mental retracing—*Starbucks on the corner; a block further down, a tall grey building with massive brass doors*—as you learn your way around an unfamiliar area.

You can recall an individual word by forming a mental picture. Visualizing a shape for the word can suggest the number of letters or syllables, or the word's general appearance. This memory tool is sometimes useful for dealing with the "tip of the tongue" problem when you know you know the word but just can't recall it. It may seem like a silhouette. For example, you might be trying to think of a word for footstool. You think it has three parts with tall letters in the middle. The silhouette is roughly

Suddenly you realize that the word is ottoman.

A mental image can also help in recalling a name. Suppose the place name you are seeking is a two-part word with a suffix beginning with the letter h like _____heim or _____hill. Then you remember it is _____ham. Once you recall the correct suffix, you may realize the name is Stoneham.

Until now, an auditory trace for Stoneham may have been the only memory trace you've had. This experience will provide a visual cue to make the name more memorable. However, if you wrote it down you would have two more cues: a kinesthetic cue from the writing itself and a visual cue from reading what you wrote.

To create a different mental picture for Stoneham, you might imagine a small stone resting on top of a whole ham. The silly quality of the association will appeal to your sense of humor, and something amusing is often well remembered.

Use Words

Some people are more apt to think in words than in pictures and seem to recall verbal or written information more readily. For instance, in following directions for operating a new clock-radio, these people would focus on the instructions rather than the diagrams.

Even if you tend to be more of a visual than a verbal person, using words is a useful tool for collecting memory traces. In planning your day, verbal reminders—either silent, aloud, or both—may be helpful as you look at your calendar.

- "Eight o'clock, call the plumber. Can he come tomorrow?"
- "Twelve o'clock, lunch with Mary."
- "Pick up cleaning and milk on the way home."
- "Four o'clock, stew on for early dinner."
- "Seven o'clock, council meeting."

Another opportunity to use words to create memory traces is to talk to yourself, silently or aloud, as you do simple tasks. If you are putting away important papers and want to be sure you can find them later, you might say:

- "Birth certificate in certificates file, but with my passport till it's renewed."
- "Oops, checkbook in the left hand drawer."
- "Electric bill with other bills to be paid."

Repeating significant words can keep you in touch with what you plan to do shortly. "Six o'clock, stove off," you might say as you set the table.

You can create a verbal tracing by talking to yourself as a reminder of how to get from here to there. In looking at a map of a strange area, you might tell yourself, either silently or aloud, "To Sharon Street, first right on Erie, second left on Rosemary, and right again on Winston. Winston runs into Sharon."

Verbal retracing is going back over where you have been in words. After losing a Mastercard you might think, Let's see, where have I been? The hardware store, and before that the laundry, and before that the grocery. Used the card at Safeway. Must be there.

Chet Parker described a verbal memory tool he developed in the Army—a reminder about the many things he was required to carry.

> "I was responsible for carrying a number of things during the day," he says, "and I was always afraid of putting one or more down and forgetting them when I left. The way I remembered was to say to myself something like 'six things.' Then as I got up to leave, I counted what I was taking and used the process of elimination to figure what, if anything, was missing. While my buddies were all getting in trouble for forgetting things, I never did."

He still uses this strategy to remember errands and shopping items which are sometimes easy to forget.

An interrupted routine is another time when a few words can be helpful. If the telephone rings while you're preparing a stew, a fast reminder, "next basil and oregano," can keep the stew from being over- or under-seasoned.

Words, as a memory tool, may also be useful in recalling a name on the tip of your tongue. If in the past you learned it well, the vagrant will usually come to mind eventually. However, if you choose to search for it, any of the following may be helpful:

- Run through the alphabet either silently or aloud: "A-, B-, C-, D-, E-, F-, G-. . . that's it, Gordon."
- Sound out the word. Suppose you think the name sounds like "cook," but that isn't quite right. You can

try out "Coke, cope, Cole, cork . . . aha, Koch."
• Repeat key words or thoughts. If you are searching
  your memory bank for the name of a man, you might
  think: I'm sure I know him. He was saying something
  about the college. Oh yes. . . the college employment
  service—a student who did such a good job painting
  his patio. Suggested I get a student to paint my fence.
  I remember now. Charlie Desmondhe was wearing a
  wild purple shirt with a parrot on the back.

Using an acronym, a phrase, or a jingle may also be helpful in
remembering a collection of items. Some people recall the names of
the Great Lakes by "HOMES," the acronym for Huron, Ontario,
Michigan, Erie, and Superior.

Many people recall the number of days in a month with: "Thirty
days has September, April, June, and November. All the rest have thirty-
one, except February with twenty-eight and twenty-nine in leap year."

Adding a word here and there can make a rhyming jingle out of
what you're working to master. This can be especially helpful for a long
series of items. Students of English history master the long succession
of rulers with the rhyme beginning, "First William the Norman, then
William his son. Henry, Stephen, Henry, Richard, and John. . . ."

A fruitful memory exercise is to develop such a rhyme for
American presidents or perhaps the sequence of streets in a city
you're about to visit. You may want to start with half the presidents
or limited sections of the city.

The sequence should be in a logical, rather than random, order.
The logic may be in terms of time, such as kings or presidents, of
space such as streets running from north to south, or of an acronym
similar to HOMES.

Repeating the acronym, phrase, or jingle from time to time will deposit it more securely in your memory bank. In addition to making information available when needed, this is an excellent exercise for improving memory in general.

Make Connections

Your memory bank is organized by logical and meaningful connections between new material and previously stored data. Every connection you make creates a memory trace to help you recall a person, object, incident, or idea.

Some connections occur naturally and without effort as you sense and respond to the world around you. Examples are:

- *W* and *o* are the first two letters in both wool and worsted, which is a firm textured woolen.
- A picture may be described as having been painted in the style of the French Impressionists.
- Your friend tells you that, while a certain congressman is a Republican, he has voted consistently with the Democrats.

Much learning takes place during the intentional search for connections between new information and what you already know. Learning is simply seeking to remember, and these kinds of connections are a big part of the process.

Two kinds of connections are important memory strategies: connections you discover and connections you create.

DISCOVER CONNECTIONS

Developing a mind-set of looking for connections will help you to remember whom and what you choose. While studying French Impressionist painting, you might confuse the names of Claude Monet and Edouard Manet. In looking for a way to remember them, you might note that each has the same vowel prominent in his first and last names. For instance, there is an *a* and an *a* sound in both Edouard and Manet. In the name Claude Monet, the *au* in French is pronounced *o*, similar to the *o* in Monet. Discovering a connection between vowels in the first and last names provides a way of recalling the men's names correctly.

Adjusting clocks properly for daylight saving time is easy if you recall that time "springs forward" in the spring and "falls back" in the fall.

Getting acquainted with strangers and learning their names is a challenge to many people. Discovering connections is a valuable tool for meeting this challenge. The process consists of asking yourself such questions as:

- Who does he look like? A friend? Someone in the news?
- Does his name suggest:
  a person
  a place, such as York, Paris, or Ireland
  a thing, such as stone, bacon, or forest
  a profession, such as miller, mason, or teller?

This thought process, which can be rapid, provides the additional memory traces needed to make a person memorable, even if there is no perfect connection. If you practice this often enough, it will become a habit that kicks in every time you meet someone new.

Remembering the content of reading material also will be easier with a mind-set of looking for connections. This involves asking questions such as:

- How does this fit into what I already know?
- In what ways is it new or different?
- What are its meaning and implications for the future?
- How can I use it?

You can look for cause and effect, or similarities and differences between this person, this object, this event, this place, this idea, and others of a similar nature that you have known. You can make associations in time or space or in abstractions like belief systems.

An experience John Blackwood had shows how discovering connections when reading helps integrate new information into one's memory bank.

Twenty-five years ago, when he was 11 years old, John lived for a year in Athens. Since he was being sent there on business for a few months, he wanted to read something about Greece that was more than a guide book. He was glad to find *Hellas, a Portrait of Greece,* by Nicholas Gage.

John read with two goals. First, he wanted to discover how present-day Greece is similar to or different from his childhood memories of the country and, second, he hoped to learn more about Greek history and culture to satisfy his own curiosity and help him relate easily to his Greek business associates.

John remembered how friendly the Greeks used to be toward Americans but had heard that America's failure to take a stand against the Turkish invasion of Crete in 1974 had changed that attitude. While reading Gage's book, he was able to connect his knowledge of America's inaction to the Greek perception that the United States wished to keep Turkey as a buffer in the Middle East. He decided to avoid political discussions which might affect the success of his business negotiations.

John had connected information he already had to the new information he learned from the book, thought about the implications of this combined information and decided on the action he should take because of it. Due to the connections he made, it was likely John would remember not to venture into a political discussion.

Also, while reading Gage's book, John looked for information about leisure time activities. He made connections between what he learned about classical ruins and his childhood memories of them and then identified familiar and unfamiliar sites he might visit.

John was glad to read that Floka's, a restaurant he remembered well, was still in existence. He made a mental note to dine there.

The discovered connections John made between his childhood experiences, his interests as an adult, and the information in Gage's book contributed greatly to his retention of what he had read.

CREATE CONNECTIONS
Sometimes there are no easy or obvious associations, but creating your own connections can help. This is particularly useful in matters having to do with daily living because you can design connections to meet specific needs. This involves making a habit of associating a time

or event with what you want to remember. For example:

- You plan to buy a new hammer at the hardware store and so picture yourself asking the manager how to repair a broken latch.
- You connect Sunday morning breakfast with filling the bird feeder.
- You tell yourself that turning on the car ignition offers a good time to check the gas gauge.

Creating meaningful connections between one thing and another is a natural way of remembering and of organizing your thinking.

Form Groups

You can recall large numbers of items by sorting them into groups with subgroups as needed. This process is called chunking.

Research has shown that the process of grouping strengthens the memory. In one project when participants were asked to make simple lists of items they were trying to recall, their memory scores improved by almost twenty-nine percent. However, when participants in a similar test were asked to make lists and then group the items, their memories improved by more than sixty percent.

In making shopping lists, you can group such items as dairy products, canned goods, cleaning supplies, and produce. If the produce group contains more than seven items (the limit of your short term memory), creating subgroups of fruit and vegetables will help you remember everything. Now, even if a distraction causes you to leave the list at home, chances are your ability to recall the items will be remarkably complete.

The effectiveness of grouping as a memory tool is a natural result of having created a variety of memory traces in the process.

A more complex grouping is demonstrated in Jane Howell's plan for a trip she wanted to take.

Jane had been studying Italian Renaissance art and planned to spend two weeks in Italy. She decided to go through her books and class notes and make a list of the buildings, paintings and statues she wanted to see. Then she grouped them by location and starred those she wanted to study at length. Next she counted each starred item as three, and totaled the numbers for each city. The sums showed what proportion of time to allot to each location.

Using this scheme, she planned to spend five days in Florence, four in Rome, three in Venice, and a day each in Assisi and Urbino. She would fly into Rome and work her way north.

In this case, Jane grouped by:

- city
- importance of art works
- number of items in each city

Grouping helped her remember what she wanted to see in each location and acted as a rehearsal for each day of the trip.

Time spent analyzing and sorting information into groups is an important part of training your memory. The more practice you have using your working memory in this way, the more efficient it will become in other areas of your life because memory skills are transferable.

Employ Repetition

Repetition is critical to the memory process because it strengthens and reinforces all other memory tools. Repetition helps you to hold information in your short term memory as your working memory organizes and integrates it into long term memory.

Repetition often is the primary tool in remembering names of strangers. Names are particularly difficult to recall when no concrete picture, meaning, or connection comes immediately to mind. When this happens, you may find that repetition is the most effective tool.

One strategy for learning a name is to accumulate a variety of memory traces: listen to it, say it, hear yourself saying it, think it, visualize it, write it down, and read it. Such repetition will help to make the name familiar. In the interim, some association may arise which will reinforce your memory of the name. For instance, you may discover in the course of a conversation that Mrs. Deerfield often has deer visiting her yard.

Learning telephone numbers provides another example of how repetition works. If you dial an unfamiliar number and find it busy, by repeating it, either silently or aloud, you can hold it in your short term memory to try again and again and again if you choose. In this way you even could keep it in mind until you went to sleep.

However, when your attention is drawn elsewhere, this memory trace will usually disappear unless you have used some other memory tool to reinforce it. For example, you might note an association between the prefix for a phone number and the rest of it, such as 501 and 1050.

In general, the more repetition there is of words, names, items, events, and ideas, the better they are stored in long term memory and the easier they are to recall.

Rehearse and Review

Rehearsal of future commitments and review of past events are important ways of building and reinforcing your memory of them. These two tools help to store and retrieve information and are strengthened by repetition.

You are using rehearsal when, the first thing in the morning, you plan a day from your calendar.

- You look at the schedule for the day, then turn away and visualize the page and its entries
- repeat the entries in your head
- tie events to each other
- include any associations which come to mind.

Review of an event is also an important memory tool. This works best if the first review is soon after the event itself. For example:

As Calvin Knowland left the Disaster Preparedness Committee meeting, he ran over the decisions they had made. Everyone agreed, he thought, that getting people prepared for any disaster was really important because the earthquake fault line was so close to town.

He was glad they had decided to get the homeowners' associations involved since the chairmen were close to what was needed in their neighborhoods. They knew who would be good volunteers and who would be at home during the day.

Calvin reminded himself, I said I'd get them off a letter first thing tomorrow. I'll describe last night's meeting and invite them to a joint session in two weeks.

Yes, he thought, tonight was a good meeting. I really believe we can make the plan work.

Calvin is reinforcing his memory of the meeting through:

- a review of the proceedings
- thoughts about the key role of the homeowners' associations
- a commitment to draft the letter
- enthusiasm about the project

Calvin would be taking advantage of another memory tool that evening when he described the meeting to his wife and again the following day as he wrote the letter. Thus, he would be spacing his review.

Space Your Repetitions

Leaving time intervals between sessions of repetition increases the effectiveness of both rehearsal and review. Bits of leisure or waiting time offer opportunities for doing so. This is what Caroline Lowell decided to do.

Caroline was looking forward to a month in Spain where she would be exchanging houses with a Spanish couple. By hook or by crook, she thought, I'm going to learn Spanish before I leave. I don't want to feel stressed out by language problems.

Yet she wondered how on earth she would find the time. As she looked at her weekly schedule, she noticed that throughout there were short periods of time in which she did nothing but wait—waiting for her grandson to come out of school, in doctor's offices, and in line at the supermarket and the toll plaza. She decided that at times like these she would listen to language CDs instead of feeling bored and irritated.

Caroline followed through on her decision and did additional spacing by spending time every evening with a Spanish grammar book. She was pleased to discover she was picking up Spanish much faster than she'd expected.

Spacing is particularly useful for learning new material when that material, such as a language or complex historical data, consists of many details that seem only loosely interrelated. As in all learning, making connections with what you already know creates new memory traces. In your spaced sessions, reminding yourself of those connections will reinforce your memory.

In addition to the memory tools we have discussed, the effective use of memory aids is often necessary to assist in recalling important items in your life.

Use Memory Aids

Memory aids are objects you use to help you remember, and they contribute greatly to the sense of being in control of your memory and your life. These are so much a part of family and school life that many people arrive at adulthood with a full repertoire: calendars, memo pads, lists, timers, tape recorders, address and record books, and pads of stick-it notes.

An important aspect of your memory project is to take charge of these memory aids. This involves identifying which would make your life more pleasant and secure, and then obtaining these aids and using them.

There is a nearly endless number of uses for memory aids.

- A timer may free you to think about something interesting during a routine task.
- "Kitchen Witches," colorful little stuffed toy witches on broomsticks, are designed to carry with you as a reminder that something is cooking on the stove.
- Notes, handy reminders that enable you to organize your life, may be a single word or pages long. For her trip to Italy, Jane made extensive notes on the art she planned to see, together with the specific qualities and techniques she was looking for. They were essential to the success of her trip.
- A journal may contain important dates and the events of each day. These may include special moments of challenge, triumph, grief, or joy; records of illnesses and inoculations, or people you have met and significant information about them. If you expect to use your journal as an effective memory aid, no matter what you decide to include, you need to devise a plan and establish a habit of making regular entries.
- Placing something impossible to forget with something you want to remember is a common memory aid. An example is putting your car keys on top of letters to be mailed since you won't leave the house without the car keys.

Memory aids for some items must be foolproof. For example, to remember your medicine, a pill safe or other device, must always be where you see it at the appropriate time. Pill safes, ranging from small to large and complex, are available to meet any pattern of medication, daily, weekly or monthly. In view of the critical need for some kinds of medication and the potency of many modern drugs, the use of such a device is a wise choice.

If many events, thoughts, or feelings are in conflict for your attention, expanding your use of memory aids will prevent significant memory lapses and contribute to your sense of being in control.

Combine Memory Tools

As you have probably already discovered, memory tools usually work together. Once again, let's use remembering names as an illustration.

Sensory awareness enables you to hear the name, see the person in the current context, listen to his conversation, sense his energy level, and become aware of your intuitions about him.

A mental image will help in reviewing his appearance. Practicing his name by using it and repeating it in your mind will keep you aware of it as you talk together. Later you can think about your conversation and space the review of what you have learned about him and what he has said.

Useful associations and connections may include his beliefs, interests, experiences, hobbies; his membership in any group, mutual friends, and topics of the conversation or activities you shared.

Making a journal entry on your meeting works as a useful memory aid for review of your meeting, and provides information for a rehearsal before meeting him the next time.

Exercises:
Memory Tools for Memory Power

Increasing Sensory Awareness

1. Select a period during each day or week to become an observer. Think of yourself as a detective or a fiction writer collecting material for a book. Tune in to your senses to assemble information on people, places, objects, and events.

2. Take a walk in a park or forest.

- What appeals to your senses? Consider sizes and shapes of the trees and shrubs, the colors of the foliage or wild flowers.
- How do you experience the ground underfoot? Is it hard and dry, or soft and muddy? Cushioned with pine needles? Crunchy with dry grass and fallen leaves?
- Do you catch the scent of pine or the fragrance of spring, summer, or fall foliage?
- Is the air still, or is there a breeze on your face?
- What parts of this experience do you enjoy most? (Feelings will reinforce this memory.)

3. Select an event such as a party, a club meeting, or a reunion with old friends, where, if possible, some of the people are strangers.

- What are your sensory impressions of the setting?
- What do you notice about each individual you talk with?

Developing Mental Images
1. In a store or market, practice creating mental pictures.

- Look at a person. Now look away and get a mental image of what you have seen. Notice distinctive features, facial expressions, gestures, and general appearance. (You can do this without staring, so no one feels uncomfortable.)
- Repeat this with two people.
- Then visualize each of them again.
- What can you intuit about these people from the mental pictures you have of them?

2. Spend some time looking at paintings in an art gallery or museum.

- Note the composition of the picture and the use of color, light and shadow.
- Observe techniques the artist has used to portray the subject. Are the brush strokes fine and delicate, or has the artist painted with a broad brush or a palette knife? How has color been used?
- Is there a special mood in the picture? How was this created?
- Does this picture evoke a feeling in you?
- Go through this process with one picture at a time. Then look away and visualize it. Repeat this at least three times with each painting.
- Note the increasing number of things you observe with repetition.

3. Locate a map of a nearby town which is unfamiliar to you. Select a public building on the map.

- Create a mental picture of the route you would take to reach it.
- See if you can go there without having to check your map in route.

As you repeat this in other areas your skill will increase.

Using Words
1. Do you tend to remember best if you think in terms of words or pictures?
2. Did you use verbal directions in addition to a mental picture in finding your way to the public building in the last exercise?
3. Be aware when a word or name is on the tip of your tongue, but you can't quite recall it.

- Do you search for it? In your head? In a dictionary or thesaurus? Or do you wait for it to come to you?
- Do you feel annoyed or anxious? Or how do you avoid these negative feelings?
- When you do remember a word you've had trouble recalling, create a new memory trace to help you recall it in the future.

4. For a week, keep track of the kinds of messages you give yourself which help you remember. Which kinds of messages do you find most useful? least useful? How might you use this information?

Making Associations and Connections

1. Using a telephone book, see how many names you can find that connect to someone or something with which you are familiar. e. g. , Forest with a forest, Smith with a blacksmith,Milton with the poet.

2. In the telephone book, look at names for which you can find no obvious connection. Can you identify some word or phrase which each sounds like? If not, take some time to repeat them to give yourself practice in learning unfamiliar names. As you do so, you may find that some association will occur to you spontaneously.

3. In keeping up with the news from Washington, note similarities and differences between current and past political figures, their styles, their voting, and their goals.

4. In your daily routine, look for connections you can make which will help you remember. Tell yourself something similar to: When I am attending the lecture at the college, I will stop in the office to pick up a course catalogue.

5. Can you create connections which would prevent the memory lapses you identified in the first exercise in Chapter One?

Grouping

1. Make a shopping list of twenty-five items.

- Sort the items into no more than six groups.
- Copy them in the sequence in which you would approach them at the store.
- Review the list just before you enter the store.
- Put it away and shop from memory.
- Look at your list before checking out to insure that you have forgotten nothing.

If you find you have forgotten quite a few items, keep repeating the process and see how practice increases your skill.

Repetition

1. Make a list of telephone numbers you use frequently but which you always look up. Learn a few of them.

- Did you learn them by repetition?
- If not by repetition, which memory tool did you use?

Rehearsal and Review

1. Select an article or book which adds to information you already have on a topic which interests you.

- Decide what new information you want to learn.
- Bear your objectives in mind as you read the material.
- Review what you have read and estimate how well your goals have been met.

Spacing Your Practice

1. How might you use spacing in the last exercise?

Using Memory Aids

1. Observe how and when you use memory aids.

2. List memory lapses from the past which you want or need to prevent. Which memory aids would prevent those memory lapses?

THREE

Find the Motivation and Commit Yourself

I F YOU HAVEN'T DONE SO ALREADY, now is the time to commit yourself. You are going to spend a little bit of each day on your own memory project. You are going to do this not only to improve your memory, but to enrich the quality of your everyday life.

Judy Morris had been a school teacher for many years. She had recently learned of a need for instructors in inner city schools to teach children who spoke English as a second language.

She thought it must be difficult for children to get their basic education in a strange language. She decided to try to help out.

When Judy's application to transfer was accepted, she began to worry. She asked her husband Bob, "How am I ever going to remember all those strange-sounding names? I've never been very good at names anyway. I hope I'm not too old to learn."

"Of course you're not," Bob said. "Give yourself time to think about it. You'll come up with something."

By the next morning, Judy had a plan. "First, I'll seat the children alphabetically and make a seating chart," she told Bob. "Then, I can see each child's name as I look at him. After that, I'll make up some get-acquainted games. Some of the students probably don't know each other, so that will help us all."

She thought she was pretty good at focusing on children one at a time. But she figured she could also practice each child's unfamiliar name in her head as she looked at the child. That was certain to help.

When we're motivated, we develop plans and concentrate on our goals. Judy's attention to her goal of learning each child's name exercised her memory tools and prompted her to make up the seating chart as a memory aid.

Ask yourself what you hope to accomplish with a better memory. The answer may be as simple as not misplacing your eyeglasses or as complex as obtaining a law degree. Then set this as your goal and keep it in mind as you work to improve your memory.

Exploit Your Own Natural Resources

Working toward goals often requires using personal resources in new ways. *In Passion for Life: Psychology and the Human Spirit*, Muriel and John James, on the basis of twenty years of research, have identified seven personal strengths or natural resources that help people reach their goals. Unlike natural resources in the environment, these increase and become more productive with use. They are:

- hope
- courage
- curiosity
- imagination
- enthusiasm
- caring and concern
- openness

Judy's commitment to her project meant she mobilized herself to get to know the children and help them learn their new language. Such a challenging task could expand her use of all of these strengths.

Hope and *courage* supported her as she faced her class determined to succeed in her job. She used *imagination* in designing games for the children. She *cared* for the children and felt *concern* for their growing up in a strange land. She was *enthusiastic* about the job and *open* to dealing with whatever challenge she encountered.

As you feel challenged to improve your memory, hope and courage will reinforce your commitment of time and energy.

Curiosity can impel you to see how the insights and exercises in this book apply to you personally and to explore in depth new fields of study that interest you. Imagination will help you to create mental pictures, think in unfamiliar ways, and design memory aids which will be tailored for you. Enthusiasm will help keep you energized as you pursue more ways of improving your memory.

Caring about people can motivate you to really listen and to respond so you will remember conversations and experiences you have shared. Concern may deepen your interest and involvement in issues of family, community, or world importance and make related information easy to recall.

Openness will enable you to expand your understanding and aid in the acceptance of new ideas. This will make people, events, and issues more memorable.

Committing yourself to make greater use of these natural resources and to using them in new ways will provide you with opportunities to increase your memory skills and your sense of personal effectiveness.

The Source of Motivation

According to the Jameses, the motivation to embark on any project results from one or more of seven deep-seated urges for something more, something better. They come from your inner self. The urges radiate energy through the mind and body to move you toward your goals.

Identify What Motivates You

Muriel and John James have identified seven basic urges which motivate people to strive toward goals. This motivation occurs at any time of life.

THE SEVEN URGES

The urges are: *to live, to be free, to enjoy, to understand, to create, to connect,* and to *transcend.*

- The urge to live is the most basic, it motivates people toward three goals on a continuum: survival, comfort, and finding meaning in living.
- The urge to be free pushes people toward the goal of self-determination. They yearn to take charge of their lives.
- The urge to enjoy motivates them to seek happiness.
- The urge to understand makes them seek knowledge.
- The urge to create energizes people toward originality, to express themselves in their unique way.
- The urge to connect pushes people to search for love and relationships with others.

- The urge to transcend moves people toward becoming more than they currently are, to grow toward personal wholeness, and to be in union with something greater than themselves.

Your desire to improve your memory no doubt relates directly to one or more of these basic urges. Ask yourself which play a part in your motivation to improve your memory skills.

Identify Energy Problems

The amount of energy available to fuel your motivation may be unnecessarily low. The Jameses have used the metaphor of a river to show how personal energy functions. The energy in the flow of water takes the river toward its destination. Three things interfere with this flow. They are: *dams, drains,* and *constrictions.*

When this metaphor is seen in terms of the flow of personal energy, comparable problems appear.

DAMS

Barriers to energy flow or blockages of energy may be created by your culture or as the result of life experiences. Discrimination against women is built into some cultures. Even in the United States, women are still fighting uphill battles against sexism in some business and academic settings.

Ageism, the prejudice and discrimination against older people, has permeated many aspects of life in our youth-oriented culture. Although this is somewhat less common than in the past, people do still experience it in the work place and the academic world, as well as in some social situations. This type of discrimination is expressed in the discounting statement, "He's too old to learn."

The fear of personal aging may generate distaste for older people. Some men and women just do not want to be reminded that everyone ages. Thus they do not want to be around "those old fogies."

You need to be clear in your mind about your attitude toward your own aging. Like most of us, if you had a choice, you probably would prefer to remain at some ideal age. However, discounting yourself because of age is a form of self-discrimination by which you create your own barriers.

Recalling the benefits of your years of experience with the resulting gains in wisdom helps you to maintain a positive self image. This is a fine gift you owe yourself. Each day of life is so precious that clouding it by moaning about things you cannot change is downright wasteful.

Financial problems create barriers to an energized life style. Widows and widowers of any age can experience severe reductions in income. Excessive medical expenses can create instant poverty. Financial problems affect such important aspects of daily living as nutrition, social contacts, and ways of spending time, all of which affect the quality of living and the motivation to remember.

Physical disability or illness is another barrier for people of all ages. Physical problems may prevent you from getting a job, living independently, or being part of a social group. Each of these presents potential obstacles to a robust memory.

Any of these barriers may leave you with little inclination to devote the attention and thought necessary to maintaining a good memory. It is important to take steps to remove or reduce these barriers and to learn to adjust your lifestyle to alleviate their impact when removal or significant reduction is not possible.

DRAINS

Drains which dissipate energy are a second problem of energy flow. Challenging tasks are grist for your memory mill, but overwork—either paid or volunteer—depletes your energy. A resulting problem may be memory lapses

If you recognize that the cause of memory problems is sometimes having too much on your schedule you then need to find ways to minimize work pressures and/or build more rest and relaxation into your free time. The problem may be alleviated simply by saying no from time to time, particularly if you realize that saying yes too often leaves you feeling drained.

Some responsibilities are not optional. Care-giving to an invalid spouse or raising orphaned grandchildren are responsibilities that often drain energy. Alzheimer's disease is particularly taxing for care-givers because it makes steadily increasing demands. People who have jobs in addition to such responsibilities may have trouble juggling their time. Memory lapses are a common complaint.

Fortunately, in many cities there are programs that provide advice and support. Day care centers offer activity programs and provide respite for caregivers. Many communities have nursing homes to provide for special needs.

If responsibilities such as these are affecting your energy level, contact one or more of these programs to investigate what they offer. Often you can locate them by browsing the Yellow Pages, checking with a member of the clergy or counselor, or contacting your local Office on Aging.

CONSTRICTION

A frequent energy problem is constriction. Constriction often stems from worry, anxiety, fear, or guilt. These feelings may be so personally overwhelming that you feel virtually immobilized. When you find yourself in what you view as a hopeless-helpless position, you may remain stuck with these feelings and not see that your problems are solvable—at least to one degree or another. The belief that there is no value in any action whatsoever is a defeatist attitude that depletes personal energy.

Develop a habit of looking for the many positive things in your life. When you find your attention is absorbed by negative feelings, consider making an "attitude adjustment" or an immediate change in your behavior. Take a walk, start on that disorganized sock drawer you've been meaning to tackle, or call up an old friend. You'll soon find you're better able to focus and concentrate on more pleasant things, and, with this, your memory functioning will automatically improve.

Eleanor Niemann experienced all three of these energy problems.

A frail lady in her early sixties, Eleanor came into a memory class complaining of several problems. She said she forgot to pay her bills and often forgot the names of old friends. She lost things, especially her purse. Her husband, until his death two years before, had taken complete charge of their son Charles, a mildly retarded adult.

When her husband died, Eleanor gave up seeing her friends and going to the synagogue because Charles had become angry and rebellious. He blamed her for his father's death and addressed her as "you bad woman." He was big and muscular, and she was afraid of him. He kept getting into trouble at the local bar, and the police often had to bring him home.

Eleanor worried about what he would do next and what would happen to him when she was gone. Her doctor referred her to a male social worker who made friends with Charles and took him around to visit group homes for other mentally handicapped men. Eventually, Charles moved into one of these homes.

Eleanor has again become active in her synagogue and is enjoying friends she hadn't seen since her husband's death. She says she hasn't lost her purse or forgotten to pay her bills since Charles moved out.

The death of Eleanor's husband created a barrier to her continuing in a meaningful lifestyle. Her energies were drained by the round-the-clock responsibility for her son. They were constricted by the anxiety she was feeling about her situation, her sense of despair in dealing with Charles' behavior, and her worries about his future when she was no longer there.

For some time Eleanor had felt too helpless to take any action toward solving her problem. When she did explore her options, she began to see some hope of a partial solution at least.

The fact is, she had been procrastinating, which restricts energy. It may allow you to feel more comfortable with inaction, however, to postpone making a commitment to solve a problem creates an obstacle within yourself. When this happens, energy in the inner self lacks an outlet, and your needs go unmet. Because of the sensitivity of the brain to inner turmoil, the attention and concentration necessary to a well functioning memory are not available.

When issues are confronted realistically, your personal energy increases. You regain a sense of having control even when none of the available choices is ideal.

If you identify a barrier or dam in your own life, the next step is to consider how you might poke holes in it or reroute your energies around it.

If you feel drained by a lifestyle with an overabundance of responsibilities, look for ways of easing the stresses you feel.

If you discover that anxiety, worry, or frequent periods of the blues are limiting your personal energies, commit yourself to exploring additional options for solving or alleviating the problems and thus reducing the constrictions. These might include:

- scheduling more positive activities in every day
- sharing your feelings with friends with the goal of increasing your insight into what you're experiencing
- joining a support group or initiating such a group
- seeking an objective point of view from a professional person such as a doctor or counselor

An excellent resource for any aging-related problem is the information and referral services provided free of charge by government agencies. Many of these are listed in the resources section beginning on page 185.

Goals from the Urge to Live

The most basic need in the James model is the urge to live, with three kinds of goals: survival, comfort, and meaning.

FIGHTING FOR SURVIVAL

All living things want to survive. In the context of modern life, this motivation often shows up as health and safety issues in which memory may play a critical role. These include things like remembering to:

- wear seat belts and look for stop signs when driving

- take critical medications
- turn off heating and electrical appliances
- lock doors

Sometimes these items represent crucial challenges to memory.

John Olson's doctor told him that taking his medication twice a day was essential if he wanted to continue driving his car. John imagined the terrible impact on his life of being without a car. He would have to move from the family home which was three miles from town. And he'd have to give up his job because there was no public transportation out to the plant where he worked.

John wondered how on earth he was ever going to be able to remember to take medication twice a day. My memory's just no good any more, he thought.

He finally committed himself to a plan which he believed would absolutely prevent his forgetting the medication. He made a connection between taking the medication and something he always did twice a day: brushing his teeth in the morning and at bedtime. As reminders, he put Xs in indelible ink on his toothbrush and toothpaste and placed the medicine right next to the toothpaste.

John's plan worked. The personal strengths he used were hope and courage to tackle a critical problem, imagination in using the Xs as a reminder, and enthusiasm about his plan. He noted it in his journal and enjoyed thinking and talking about it. All this repetition ensured that he would easily remember his plan. He made a commitment and took charge of solving his problem.

DESIRING COMFORT

Once we feel safe from threats to our lives or lifestyles, we want to feel comfortable. A memory lapse is sometimes the cause of rueful amusement. However, discomfort from mislaying keys, forgetting appointments, or forgetting where you parked your car can range from minor to extreme, with possible physical, emotional, and financial repercussions. Finding yourself locked out of your car on a cold rainy night because of a memory lapse can be a crisis. In addition, it can shake your self-confidence.

A plan to keep track of such items as keys and eyeglasses typically involves selecting logical places for each, both at home and away and making habits of keeping them there.

Until your new habit is well established, you may occasionally forget and need to retrace your steps, either mentally or physically. When distracted, you may deviate from your new routine. However, your habit will become more and more dependable if the plan is logical and you continue to practice and review it.

Maria Pappas shows how this works when she tells her friend Cynthia about her success in coping with five pairs of eyeglasses.

"It seems every time I go to the eye doctor I end up getting a new kind of glasses," Maria told her friend. "I now have five pair."

"Why on earth would anyone want five pair of glasses?" Cynthia asked.

"Weird, huh! Well, for regular use I have progressive lenses like bifocals. But they distort peripheral vision. So I have reading glasses for the newspaper and distance glasses for night driving.

"I have some old reading glasses that are just right for the computer. And, of course, there are my sunglasses."

Cynthia nodded. "Makes sense. How on earth do you keep track of them?"

"It was tough. I was driving myself crazy trying to find the pair I wanted. Then I remembered something. My dad, a Navy man, used to say, 'Look sharp! Be sharp! A place for everything, and everything in its place.'"

"So I figured out where every pair should go. Sunglasses in the car visor. Night driving glasses in the glove compartment. Reading glasses on the table by my favorite chair. Computer glasses on the desk, and the progressive lenses on my nose.

"It's all completely logical, and it sure saved my sanity."

A memory lapse which causes you a lot of discomfort can be avoided if you commit to a new habit as Maria did. The more often you use your habit, the better it functions. This technique will not only solve the problem, it will improve your memory in general.

SEARCHING FOR MEANING

Closely related to the urge to live is the need to find meaning in your life. Meaning and memory are intimately related. Events with meaning are often easily recalled and well remembered. An example is something David Quimby experienced.

David shared a seat on an airplane with a volunteer from Habitat for Humanity in Americus, Georgia. He was surprised to learn that, in addition to building houses, the volunteers were working to create a sense of community in the new project. They hoped to make a safe and supportive environment for families.

For some time David had been worried about the lack of communication among various ethnic groups in his home town and the rising level of violence threatening the sense of community.

As a result, he decided to volunteer at Americus where he could learn first hand about the organization's techniques for building a sense of community and explore whether he might develop a similar program at home.

David frequently recalled this plane ride and his work in Americus as he started a program for parents and children in his own city.

In the events of every day, we are often deeply involved in issues with meaning. If you are concerned about the future of government health care, you will want to learn about and remember the various plans for preserving it and what each would mean to you and your family. The fact that this subject has meaning to you will help you remember the details of each plan.

Thinking through subjects like this often leads to a further search for information and the taking of some action. This whole process may lead you into new ways of thinking—a healthy stimulus for your brain cells and your memory.

Forgetting recent events and conversations is a frequent complaint in memory training classes. Since meaning and memory have such a close relationship, look for more meaning in everyday experiences as an aid to remembering them. This extra attention and concentration will create new memory traces. And, as we have seen, any one of these traces may help you recall a total experience. Here are some suggestions:

- Look for distinctive meanings in things you read. A book about an artist losing his eyesight can be a model of courage in dealing with adversity in any area of life. Such a book would be unforgettable if your own life called for such courage.
- While chatting with friends, look for the meaning they get out of their life experiences. Your understanding of this will make the conversation more enjoyable and more memorable.
- Look for the meanings behind the news on TV. What are the possible outcomes of a Supreme Court decision? How is an event affecting the lives of the people experiencing it?

Increasing your insight and understanding in these ways both adds to your memory store and contributes to a mind-set for improving your memory.

The second urge in the James model is a desire for freedom.

Goals from the Urge to be Free

PRESERVING SELF-DETERMINATION

Much of the deep-seated urge to be free is the need to be in charge of your life and to make your own decisions about where to live and how to spend your time.

Courage is required when a widow returns to school with students younger than her children in order to learn the skills she needs to get a job and remain independent.

It takes courage to learn the ins and outs of zoning laws and to organize your neighborhood to fight changes which would reduce the value of your property. Yet, as you strive for such goals you'll often find renewed energy which, in turn, fosters the growth of your memory skills.

The greatest threat to freedom for some mature people is loss of the ability to live independently. Health and safety issues are closely related to this freedom. When Mother and Dad seem forgetful, a loving adult child may assume they need someone else to make their decisions. Often this occurs because of incidences of memory lapses which threaten personal welfare, forgotten medication, an iron which overheats, or a pan left to burn on the stove. These incidents often provide the motivation required to make a commitment to solve memory problems.

Thelma Stetson and Sadie Talbot met in a memory training class. At the first session they discovered a common concern. Each had forgotten to turn off the fire under her tea kettle which had burned dry. Thelma's had caused a fire. Fortunately her son had given her a fire extinguisher, and she was able to put out the fire herself.

Sadie was particularly upset about her ruined tea kettle because it was a gift from her daughter Lois. It was trimmed with porcelain in Delft blue and white. She had hoped to duplicate it but couldn't find one like it anywhere at any price.

She dreaded having to tell Lois. Probably the whole family would start discussing nursing homes again the way they did when she fell and broke her arm.

A man in the class told them about an electric tea kettle that was somewhat expensive but turned off automatically.

Sadie and Thelma went shopping for tea kettles, and the following week both ladies reported their problem was solved. Despite limited financial resources, they agreed that their peace of mind was worth every cent of the price.

It takes both courage and commitment when people are struggling to remain independent and in charge of their lives.

YEARNING TO BE FREE OF NEGATIVE FEELINGS

Psychological freedom involves being free to use all your personal resources in working toward your goals. You lose psychological freedom if your thoughts and/or feelings interfere with your attention and concentration, two things which affect your ability to remember.

A positive attitude enables you to make a commitment and concentrate on working toward your objectives. In contrast, some attitudes may sabotage your memory project. Dave may think, I'll never be able to remember the different kinds of city zoning, thus discounting his own ability to learn. He might tell himself, I've always had a lousy memory. I'm too old to do anything about it now.

Dianna, a perfectionist, looks for errors. She feels stupid because she has forgotten one of the six types of city zoning. Yet she is ignoring the fact that she has just finished describing the five others in detail.

Danny, a procrastinator, worried that he won't be able to master all the ins and outs, plans to study zoning districts tomorrow or maybe next week, but by then, he will have conveniently forgotten all about it.

In addition to attitudes, natural responses to life experiences can also sabotage a memory project. A recent house fire may cause grief over lost possessions and anxiety over repair of the building. These feelings can occupy so much attention that a person mislays keys, neglects important tasks, or forgets the names of close friends.

The desire to be free from worry or fear can be a powerful motivator. Men and women with courage take charge of their lives. Frequently they choose to obtain help from a counselor. They look for ways to free themselves from overwhelming feelings and concerns. Being able to focus on troubling issues and to survey all possible solutions enables them to select those which best address their personal priorities.

Judy Usher is an example of one whose feelings had a profound impact on her memory.

In explaining why she had come into a memory training group, Judy said, "I'm sixty-eight years old, but I never felt old until I moved into this retirement community. Since I've been here, my memory has gone to pot.

"For forty years I lived in the same house on a cliff overlooking the ocean. My husband and I were so happy there.

"My daughter lives here. After her dad died, she used to drive eighty miles round trip to see me every weekend. She said she wanted to be sure I was all right. She made me feel so guilty when she complained about how hard it was for her to drive all that long way. And she kept talking about how wonderful it is here in Oakdale. Well, I don't think it's wonderful!

"Now I can't go back. My house has been sold, and I'm too old to find someplace else on the water. I just hate it here.

"You asked why I'm in this class. I'm here because I want to stop forgetting things."

Before long Judy began to suspect that her grief and anger over leaving her beloved home might be related to her forgetfulness. She later told the class she had decided to try to make the best of it in Oakdale since there was no chance of her going back home. Judy volunteered for the Seniors in the Schools program, joined a duplicate bridge club, and began to have dinner once a week with a group of women who lived alone.

About six months later, she telephoned the teacher of the memory class to say, "I want you to know that I just don't have much trouble with my memory anymore."

Working through negative thoughts and feelings increases psychological freedom even when no perfect solution to a problem is possible. Employing this healthy approach enables you to set reasonable limits on these feelings. You can focus on positive and supportive messages in contrast to the negative messages which foster depression and sabotage your memory.

If you commit to using your own natural resources, no matter what motivates you or what hurdles are in your path, your memory program will be successful.

Exercises:
Develop Your Resources and
Energy for a Better Memory

1. The following is a bar chart drawn to reflect the self-evaluation of a woman who considers herself high in hope, courage, and caring and concern, but who feels she could increase her use of the natural resources of curiosity, imagination, enthusiasm, and openness.

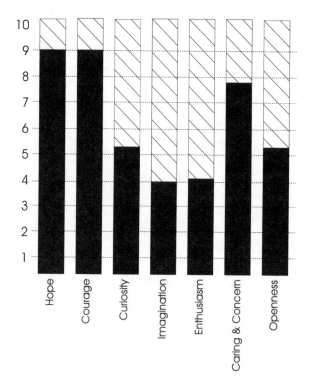

Evaluate your use of these seven natural resources in your life by sketching a bar chart like the one above. Blacken in each bar to the extent you feel you use the resource. Indicate the ones you would like to increase your use of by crosshatching above the filled-in area on the appropriate bars.

In what ways might each of these qualities be useful in improving your memory? How might you use one or more of them in a new way this week?

2. In which of these areas of your life do you want to improve your memory:

- Health and safety?
- Comfort?
- Physical freedom?
- Psychological freedom?

3. Which natural resources in Exercise 1 on the previous page will help you in each area you identified? How and when might you use them?

FOUR

Enjoy Life and Continue to Grow

According to *PASSION FOR LIFE* authors Muriel and John James, other basic urges which motivate people are: to enjoy, to understand, to create, to connect with others, and to transcend or to do or be more than we were previously. Motivation plays an important role in improving memory because working toward a goal fosters attention and concentration. These in turn help to make the necessary memory traces. This is true regardless of which urges have priority at any particular time.

Learn to be Happy

People easily remember events which they have enjoyed.

> Nancy and Dick Vernon were reminiscing about Christmas in their old home. Nancy said, "Do you remember when Dad used to hang the sheet over the door to the living room so we wouldn't see Santa Claus. And how we used to sit on the stairs and listen to see if we could hear him?"
>
> "And how exciting it was when dad took down the sheet and we saw the tree with all the lights and the presents," Dick added.
>
> "I used to love it when our uncles came for Christmas. They were so much fun. You could always count on them for great

family stories."

"Do you remember the one about Great Grandpa Smith cheating at cards?" Dick asked. "When someone would catch him at it, Grandma always scolded him, and said, 'Now, John, you must be a good example for the children.' And he would say, 'You have to teach them to watch out for those card sharps. If they don't learn at home, where will they learn?'

Nancy laughed. "And Grandma would say, 'Tut tut, John. You know better than that. You just want to win.' Then he would wink at us children and say, 'Of course, dear, you're always right.'"

"I don't know how many times I've heard that story," Dick said, "but I always laugh. Grandpa was so big and tall with his mop of black hair and bushy eyebrows. And Grandma was so tiny, she had to look up to talk to him. What a pair!"

This is the sort of happy reminiscing that can continue like links in a chain when families get together.

Everyone has experienced the urge to enjoy. It's as natural as breathing, and the events you enjoy deeply are easy to recall. Happy occasions such as weddings, births of children, first jobs, promotions, and major accomplishments become fine, easily recalled memories. Talking with relatives or friends who also enjoyed those experiences will kindle half-buried memories. The more you share, the more you'll be able to recall.

DECIDE TO ENJOY

If everybody wants happiness, why don't we experience it more often?

For the perfectionist, memories of past failures may block the desire to enjoy. Disappointments, low self-esteem, or guilt can inter-fere with feelings of pleasure. In such cases, you need to increase self-acceptance for who you are now, taking into consideration that you are a growing person who can learn from your mistakes without berating yourself for making them. This, along with focusing on past and future accomplishments, can free the urge to enjoy.

Grief often clouds the days of those who have suffered the loss of a loved one, a cherished home, or another significant part of their lives. Spending time with a friend for support can help you to move through these difficult times. You might try to balance your sadness with a happy memory related to the person or possession you have lost. This may not abolish grief, but a little distance from the pain provides space for the emergence of new insights and different ways of thinking. Coming to terms with grief, sometimes with professional counseling, can help you find increasing satisfaction and happiness in here-and-now living.

Many people have periods of feeling just plain blue. Good first-aid for the blues is to pay attention to all the little opportunities for enjoyment in everyday events: the bright blue sky after a week of rain, a chance meeting with an old friend, hummingbirds hovering among the trumpet vines, the laughter of children. A habit of noticing and recalling such small delights will improve the quality of your life as well as your memory.

Seek Knowledge

Most of us want to know and understand more about ourselves and our world. This urge can surface at any time as simple curiosity which may be the first step in creating a whole new network of memories. For example, the development of your personal philosophy may lead you to explore the thinking of philosophers down through the ages. Recognition that philosophy cannot be well understood without knowledge of the context within which it evolved can lead to a concern with the cavalcade of history.

Motivated to learn more about the world in which she lives, Betsy Evans and her friend Dorothy often begin informal study projects.

Betsy was interested in volcanoes. "I've developed a passion for them," she told Dorothy. "I feel awed by all that molten lava spewed up by an incredible primal energy force five miles down in the core of the earth. It's the same energy that's been generating since the earth was formed."

"That's why I was thrilled when the pilot of a small plane offered to fly me close to Mt. Saint Helens a few years after it erupted in 1980. He circled the volcano and maneuvered the plane so close that I felt as though I could reach out and touch it. We could see the dome and smoke pouring out. It was a wonderful experience.

"And Kilauea in Hawaii is incredibly beautiful at night—a fountain of lava shooting high in the sky, with a red river of new molten rock running down the black mountain into the sea. Fantastic!"

Dorothy on the other hand, had taken an interest in finance. "I want to know more about managing money," she laughed. "Well, even if we have different interests at least we can study together."

Such study projects create new ways of thinking, which, as you know, stimulates neurons and thus increases memory power.

However, learning and understanding may sometimes be affected by difficulty in remembering material you have read or heard. The following strategies can help to solve these problems.

READING FOR PLEASURE

Reading for pleasure often involves savoring and rereading those parts that seem the most beautiful, the most inspiring, the most meaningful. Pausing from time to time, you may consider:

- what the author is describing
- how the characters feel and respond to the events in their lives
- ways they interact
- decisions they are making

You may also imagine the setting, perhaps in broad strokes as one you have seen or lived in. You may compare characters and their behavior with people you have known or contrast the story with your own life. In short, you, as the reader, contribute to the story.

Sometimes characters become role models in people's lives. A book may present a solution to a problem confronting the reader and change his perspective. Often the reader is moved out of the here-and-now into another world. It can be a memorable experience imbued with serenity, excitement, joy, or danger. Such events and activities provide new memory traces which make what you've read easier to recall.

READING FOR INFORMATION

Reading for information uses a group of skills which can be sharpened. In fact, use alone sharpens them. If you augment these skills with memory aids such as note-taking, you'll find yourself retaining more of what you read with less and less effort. This is true without regard to what you decide to study—archaeology, stamp collecting, gourmet cooking, politics, or surfing the Internet.

A practical scheme for reading to remember is the *SQ3R* plan, used in wartime to improve the reading skills of military recruits. The plan is:

- Survey—Skim the material to get an overview.
- Question—Form questions by turning headings and subheadings into questions or creating questions to which you expect to find answers as you read the text.
- Read—Read through the material focusing on what has meaning for you. Underline important points or jot them down.
- Recite—Recite what you have read by repeating the important items, preferably aloud, to collect more memory traces
- Review—Go over your notes or the material you marked. If possible, discuss them in a group, or with a friend for an active review. Spacing the review over hours or days will help establish the information securely in your memory bank.

Another useful step is to decide how you will use or build on what you have learned.

Roberta Franklin named her new business COURTESY. Its motto was, "We do anything for you that you don't want to do for yourself."

She was intrigued by the book *Promoting Your Business with Free (or Almost Free) Publicity* by Donna G. Albrecht. Roberta thought this looked like a gem for someone with only minimal capital but a service she knew would grow if she could get the word out.

Using the SQ3R system, she skimmed over the table of contents and leafed through the book reading the heads and subheads to get an idea of what was presented. She then wrote down three questions she wanted answered.

- How can I use community groups to publicize my work?
- How can I get the media to notice my service?
- How can I use my love of public speaking to develop new sales?

She read the text, jotting notes about information that interested her. When she found the answer to one of her questions, she recited it aloud to the empty room where she was studying.

That weekend, over coffee, she ran over her notes with her friend Jane who helped Roberta fine-tune a couple of ideas.

The SQ3R method worked well for Roberta. She was soon speaking on COURTESY to men's and women's groups and attracting media attention as well.

Adopting a habit of using this organized approach to reading will make a major contribution to the quality of your study and the success of your memory project.

Another strategy that will help you remember what you read is to learn what you can about:

- the background and experience of the author
- the objectives of the author in writing what you've read (Consider for yourself how well the author reached her objectives)

- the information on which the author's conclusions are based
- the implications of this new information in your life or community and what new doors it could open for more study

REMEMBERING WHAT YOU HEAR

We acquire knowledge from lectures, movies, television, and conversations. Unfortunately, most of us retain no more than twenty-five percent of what we hear. One reason is that this information is typically heard only once. Yet there are steps you can take to improve your listening-to-learn skills.

Before listening to a speech examine background data and/or design questions you want answered. This will help you to integrate new information. Other devices are:

- seek connections with what you already know
- plan to learn more about a subject
- make notes during or soon after hearing a talk
- review by thinking about the talk or by discussing it with someone else

If you and a friend plan to attend a lecture on health insurance, you might decide in advance what you want to learn and perhaps make a topic outline with space to jot down notes.

Discussing the lecture with your friend afterward enables both of you to share and to reinforce your memories, some of which may be different.

For further review, you might check out books and pamphlets from your library.

NEVER STOP LEARNING

As the urge to understand stimulates learning, memory skills grow. This is a process that can go on for life. With the phenomenal increase in knowledge in all fields and our world changing at a rapid pace, just keeping abreast in an area where you may once have been proficient is a challenge. Staying current or branching out into completely new subjects will stimulate little-used neurons and expand your memory power.

Classes at community and four-year colleges, as well as adult education programs, are easy ways to get started. With the increase in early retirement, more and more men and women are going back to school to complete their formal educations, earn graduate degrees, or explore new fields. For some, television classes prove convenient.

Universities often offer opportunities for volunteers to participate in local or even overseas research projects which offer unique learning situations along with valuable hands-on experience.

Elderhostel programs, designed for groups of people over fifty-five, are week-long courses in a residential setting. Classes are conducted by professionals in their fields and offered throughout the United States and in many foreign countries. The costs, including room and board, are remarkably low for such enriching programs, and scholarships are sometimes available. (To get on the Elderhostel mailing list, contact: Elderhostel, 75 Federal Street, Boston, MA 02110, or go online: elderhostel. org.)

Elderhostel topics cover the range of human knowledge from the arts and sciences to outlaws and river rafting to family and world history to primitive cultures and visions of the future. In addition, many classes offer hands-on training in the arts.

Express Your Originality

The urge to create may motivate you in any field of artistic endeavor as well as in other areas of life. Activities may include such things as inventing a timesaving technique on your job, helping out with a school play, creating a pleasant atmosphere in a grumpy household, or planning a fund-raiser for Meals-on-Wheels.

In every creative task, being able to remember the process of the project and all that has gone before is basic to its success. Memory is necessary to keep you in touch with your options, what you have already tried, and your plans for the future. In complex tasks, keeping notes of what you have done and plan to do is an essential memory aid.

Creativity with retirement may mean moving into a completely new field with chances to develop new memory skills. This is a period for doing things you never have had time to do, such as researching your family tree or volunteering for the Peace Corps.

Many people launch new careers in their retirement years. Some, after years of going to the office, choose to move into the arts.

Charles Yale, after thirty years as a stockbroker, trained to become a chef. He now devotes his working hours to catering gourmet meals for fund-raising galas. His specialty is creative adaptations of ethnic cuisines into dishes which are new, beautiful, and delicious.

Other men and women use their creativity by working with words. Poets and essayists, biographers and mystery writers exercise their word-sorting skills and expand their working vocabularies.

Writing your life story is a particularly meaningful way to be creative. Some men and women wish to leave their descendants a memoir which explores and explains the writer's unique life experiences and the time in which they lived.

Remembering long-past experiences generates more and more old memories. Some autobiographers have been amazed at how many long-buried memories surface as they pursue their writing. A particularly rewarding aspect of this life review process is reliving relationships with friends and relatives.

The activity inherent in being creative helps to build strong memory skills.

Develop Relationships

The urge to connect, like other urges, is in our genes. No one exists in isolation. From the time we are born, we need to feel connected to others in order to survive and be healthy. In the natural course of living each person develops relationships and seeks love.

Men and women gain from the kind of reciprocal attention which says, "You're there. You're important." When people are actively involved in providing and receiving care and concern for each other, meaningful memories are created naturally.

Yet many people in memory classes have complained about forgetting what friends—even dear friends—have told them. Such memory lapses are usually due to lack of attention, often because of distractions. The degree to which one is paying attention at any moment determines how securely the memory of that moment will be integrated into the memory bank. This will vary from time to time and person to person.

Even in close relationships, distractions interfere with attention. A common type of distraction exists when people have conflicting attitudes. Evaluating opinions and making judgments while another is talking can absorb so much of your attention that you leave little available to register much more of the conversation than the fact that there is disagreement.

In every case, your attention to people and their concerns determines your memory of them and what you have said and done together. The challenge is to take charge of where you train the spotlight of your attention.

CHANGING RELATIONSHIPS

As years pass, some longtime friends and intimates may no longer be available. Families relocate; divorce or death divides couples. Work-related relationships may fade or vanish with the job. Forming new relationships is sometimes difficult. Physical health, financial considerations, or shyness may result in a reluctance to reach out to make new friends and try new activities. Because of these factors, your social contacts can be severely limited. Feeling comfortable meeting strangers and making new friends can be a major asset as you grow older.

REMEMBERING STRANGERS AND THEIR NAMES

Here again, in connecting with new people, the ability to remember names becomes important. "I've never been any good at remembering people's names, and I'm too old to start now," is a common complaint of people in memory training groups. The belief about being "too old" is simply not true. So long as people are motivated and set their own pace, they can continue to learn. They can even learn how to learn better.

Several factors may interfere with your ability to master the names of strangers as they are introduced.

- The first is that a name is usually said just once. It lasts a second and is reinforced by an "echo" in the brain, after which it disappears. In contrast, the face, posture, appearance, and setting are there to be observed in the moments following the introduction.

- A second factor is an inability to hear the name correctly. If a series of introductions is rapid, the names may interfere with each other. A speaker may have a soft voice that prevents people with even minor hearing difficulties from catching a name.

- The third factor is inattention. You may be focusing on the person's appearance, clothing, or some other element in the environment. Or you may be trying to remember if you turned off the sprinkler system at home. Perhaps you're busy worrying about failing to remember people's names.

- A fourth factor is stress, and stressful periods do occur in life from time to time. Strong feelings like ongoing anxiety or grief make learning everything more difficult than usual.

In all of these situations, forgetting is not the issue. *The names were never learned in the first place.*

A plan for learning the names of strangers which has proved useful is to:

- STOP all other thought
- LISTEN to the name
- LOOK at the stranger
- REPEAT the name often, both silently and in conversation

A way of remembering this plan is to associate it with the "Stop! Look! Listen!" signs at rural railroad crossings. You can then remember the plan through that connection made more memorable by the different sequence of the words. Then add "REPEAT," a common memory tool.

If remembering names is important to you, simply focusing on a stranger's name as the first item of concern during an introduction enables you to begin developing this memory skill. At that moment everything else about the person should be secondary. Repeating the name, either silently or aloud, will keep it in short term memory while you are registering the person's appearance, the surroundings, and what you are discussing. In this way a number of memory traces are stored in long term memory. The name is linked to the other information and will be easier to recall.

Writing down the name and a few notes about the appearance and interests of the person after your meeting is a useful memory aid. This is particularly important if you will not see the person for some time.

These devices can be used in any social or business gathering. Spaced review of the name will help to integrate it.

FRIENDSHIP

Close relationships take time to develop, and most people have acquaintances and friends with whom they have varying degrees of intimacy.

The confidant relationship with mutual caring and sharing is a valuable asset as people grow older. The confidant acts as a buffer in coping with the grief of any loss whether physical, social, or financial. Otherwise, such losses often result in depression, a major cause of memory problems.

In confidant relationships, people feel free to share everyday joys and sorrows and to brainstorm solutions to vexing problems. People stimulating each other to explore new ways of thinking are often more productive than one person alone, especially one who has recently lost a support system. All of these activities are grist for the memory mill.

As a relationship grows more open and meaningful, it may evolve into what Muriel James has described in *The Heart of Friendship* as a "third self." She uses the metaphor of a chord, the sum total of which is more than each of the two musical notes played separately. The relationship itself is an entity which is more than two individuals. It involves a kind of personal transcendence.

Desiring Something More

The urge to transcend may be manifested in the need to become whole within oneself, to learn or experience more. Perhaps your reason for reading this book stems from a desire to transcend your memory problems. Transcendence occurs when a person is open to the personal growth and change which contribute to moving beyond his or her present reality. A sense of wholeness or unity with all of creation may be the gift of transcendence.

SPHERES OF DIALOGUE

Martin Buber, a 20th century theologian, calls the experience of transcendence "dialogue," of which he has identified four spheres.

The first is stones to stars. This is experienced when you have a sense of union with the inanimate parts of creation. You may have a special place you like to go, in fact or fantasy, where you experience a type of serenity or personal unity that is different from your everyday life.

Possibly it is on the shore of a lake or on a mountaintop or in a valley surrounded by rolling hills. In this special place, you sometimes have a sense of moving beyond yourself to be in union with the beauty around you. This is Buber's first sphere of transcendence. Such moments are etched in your memory to be recalled over and over. They decorate your life.

The second sphere is dialogue with plants and animals. When you look into the eyes of a loved pet, you two may communicate silently. Sometimes, when I have eye contact and talk with a Norwegian elkhound friend of mine, he murmurs to me from deep in his throat. Or if you talk with your plants you may have a sense of their inner beings. At such times, you feel as if you are moving beyond your everyday world. You gain precious memories in these special moments.

The third sphere is connection with an artist or creator through his work. It may happen that when you are looking at the Sistine ceiling, you meet Michelangelo. This experience is more than an intellectual analysis of what and how he painted or the appreciation of the beauty of his work. It is the sensation of his being present in the magnificence of that work. You might even "see" Michelangelo lying on his back with his brush creating that outstretched hand which gave life to man. An inspiring memory!

The fourth sphere is meeting another human being when you are fully present and open to each other. There is a mutual sharing of thoughts and concerns and each participates in the other's experience. This is in contrast to monologic conversation when each thinks of what to say next as the other is speaking.

True dialogue, as envisioned by Buber, involves no personal agenda of influencing, persuading, judging, controlling, or enhancing self-esteem. It is simply meeting the other in openness and acceptance.

Such a connection can occur when the eyes of two strangers meet across Symphony Hall during a concert and sense they are fully engaged in the music, brought together by the creation of the composer and the skills of the conductor and orchestra. In this memorable experience, inner core energies of two strangers are caught up in the same music as they experience it together.

Moments of transcendence are often recalled for a lifetime. They are powerful memories because of the experience of moving into a space beyond the limits of daily living and because of the feelings involved. These events cannot be programmed, but openness to other people and to the world around offers everyone opportunities for transcending the limits of the everyday.

The Jameses have identified a fifth sphere of dialogue, communication with your inner self when you have a sense of the many potentials within you. You somehow realize you can be more than you presently are. This seems to happen when people are deeply committed to a project and discover unexpected personal abilities. This happened to Martha Hornburg.

Martha was having memory problems and had been diagnosed as having had brain damage because of starvation in a war zone where she lived as a child. She participated in two memory courses and was fully committed to do whatever she could to use her remaining capacities to the best of her ability.

Martha decided both to work at better focusing her attention by increasing her sensory awareness of everyday activities, and to develop habits of concentration which would reduce distractions in her life. She hoped that these would reduce her memory lapses.

Martha identified her personal strengths (See the exercises in Chapter Three) and set goals for those she planned to increase—hope, curiosity, imagination, and openness.

She plotted her use of time on a pie chart. As a result, she made some decisions that would provide for a more meaningful use of her time. Her charts in bright colors and her willingness to share her experiences were an inspiration to other members of the class.

A year or so later Martha made a surprise visit to a memory class with a pot of miniature red roses. "This is a symbol of what I have done with my life since I took this class," she said.

Interacting Urges

The seven basic urges that motivate all of us make up a useful system of identifying the energies which empower you to remember and to keep improving your ability to remember.

In review, they are: the urge to live (with goals to survive, be comfortable and find meaning), the urge to be free, the urge to enjoy, the urge to understand, the urge to create, the urge to connect, and the urge to transcend. They may often work together.

The seven personal strengths of hope, courage, curiosity, imagination, enthusiasm, caring and concern, and openness also can work together to help you reach your goals.

Gloria Washburn provides an example of the rewarding way in which all the urges and personal resources can interact.

Gloria was a retired bookkeeper living in New Jersey when she had a telephone call from her Uncle Joe's lawyer in California. She had just inherited the old family home on an acre of land. The lawyer said, "Your uncle hoped that you would enjoy living there as much as he did."

Gloria faced a difficult decision. The idea of moving all the way across the country was frightening. She'd never even been out of New Jersey! Suppose I don't like California? she thought. Yet she had to admit that retirement so far had been pretty boring. Maybe that's why she kept forgetting things—nothing in her life seemed worth remembering.

The more Gloria considered her inheritance the more enthusiastic she became. It would be fun living in her mother's old home. For the first time in her life she could have a real garden like her mother's. Suddenly, the house seemed like a very special gift.

Once Gloria had moved into her new home, she bought a Sunset gardening book to learn about plants that would grow in her area, how to feed and care for them, and which would take minimum care and expense. She marked pages and made notes about plants to examine at the nursery.

Next Gloria developed a landscaping plan considering color combinations, fragrance, and growth habits of each plant. She wanted plants that would create a show in the winter months.

Gloria joined the garden club and visited other members' gardens. She found people friendly and helpful. They made her feel right at home.

One evening she thought back to the six months of her retirement she'd spent in New Jersey, and realized that back there she'd become a couch potato, planning her life around TV programs, shopping trips, and eating out once a week with Connie.

What a contrast this was to California where her life revolved around her garden and her new friends. The first thing she did every day was to go out to the yard to see how her new plants were doing.

Gloria wrote to Connie in New Jersey and told her she loved living in California! She enclosed pictures of her new garden, which, she told Connie, had given a whole new meaning to getting up in the morning.

"Not only do I love the colors and textures and fragrances of the flowers," she wrote her friend, "but I really like learning about plants. My next project will be hybridizing iris. That was my mother's hobby, and I remember what beautiful flowers she grew."

Gloria demonstrates how hope, courage, curiosity, imagination, enthusiasm, caring and concern, and openness to new ideas and experiences, can work together to help someone move into a new way of living.

She used all these natural resources as she freed herself from a humdrum existence to adopt an enjoyable and meaningful lifestyle. This involved learning new kinds of information and offered an opportunity for her to express her creativity in landscaping her property. She made new friends and developed a close and heartwarming relationship with her plants. She has become highly energized and deeply involved as she continues learning in new fields and new ways. She transcended her old way of being and adapted a new lifestyle, one that fosters a fine memory. This is the kind of activity which grows new dendrites and expands the number of synapses enabling you to learn more and to learn better.

Exercises:
Begin to Form Your Plan

1. Review your reasons for wanting to improve your memory. Have any of them changed as you have progressed through this book? Can you identify how they relate to the five urges discussed in this chapter?

2. What urges (to enjoy, to understand, to create, to connect, to transcend) have priority for you? Rate them from #1 to #5, with #1 being the highest and #5 the lowest.

3. As you look at the urges with the highest priorities, which of the seven natural resources (hope, courage, curiosity, imagination, enthusiasm, caring and concern, and openness) will help you in reaching your goals?

4. Are there additional qualities you will need? (These might include persistence, patience, and self-discipline.)

5. Each journey begins with a single step, followed by another and yet another. What will be your first, second and third steps in working toward one of your goals?

6. Answer this same question about your other goals. Will it be possible to work on two or more goals at the same time?

FIVE

Increase Your Power to Focus

Do you ever find yourself driving north on a freeway when south is the direction that would take you where you want to go?

Did you ever carefully select flowers as a gift to your hostess and discover, as you knocked on her door, that you had left them at home on the hall table?

Such experiences demonstrate that *attention* and *concentration* are basic to memory. Attention is like a spotlight moving around our inner and outer worlds focusing on a sensation here, a thought there, or a feeling somewhere else. Concentration is sustained attention which consolidates sensory data, thoughts, and feelings. It typically involves thinking in depth and using the memory tools discussed in Chapter Two.

The following episode suggests the power of attention and concentration.

After an absence of forty years, Ellen Davis has returned to a craggy headland on the Maine coast near the cottage where she spent summers as a child.

Standing on the cliff looking out to the open ocean, she muses about how much she loves this view of the surf and the sea.

She loves the wildness of this coast where the rocks jut up and out at harsh angles and gulls swoop and dive into breaking waves, where the changing sea ripples whitecaps and surges breakers in colors all the way from gray to green to deep dark blue.

She hears a watery swish as the incoming tide hits a blow hole and spouts a fountain of foam. She is amazed that the blow hole remains after so many years! A fresh wind chills her face and leaves a salt spray on her lips.

She suddenly realizes what a wonderful memory the place has been for her over the years. She's made a career of painting portraits. Now she decides to put this special place on canvas to enjoy as often as she wishes.

Ellen is deeply engrossed in the scene, which is colored by her memories of the past. This total attention and concentration will give her the many memory traces which will help her create her own vision of this scene. She will interpret the experience in a unique way by her knowledge and skills in composition, color, and creating a mood.

Like an artist memorizing a seascape, you can focus your attention and concentrate on whatever it is you want to remember. This requires being tuned into the information smells, sights, sounds that your senses are gathering, thinking about the experience, and recognizing what you feel about it.

Katy Reynolds' experience in shopping for a new car is another example of this process at work.

Katy was checking out a new model she was seriously considering. In order to remember this particular car, she paid attention to the information her senses were supplying her.

Her kinesthetic sense, through her skin and muscles, delivered information about the car's ease of handling and its comfort. Visual information concerned her ability to see the road front and rear and the car's color and styling. She also perceived other visual data on the window sticker and in the descriptive pamphlet. Auditory information included the noise of operation and the information given to her by the salesman.

Her thoughts dealt with information pertaining to whether the car's size, price, warranty, and maintenance history seemed reasonable and satisfactory. She compared it with other models and makes she'd seen and wondered whether another dealer might have this car for less money.

Input from her emotions included feelings about having a new car, about the color and style of this one, anxiety about her old car, worry that she might be spending too much money, and her assessment of the salesman's marketing style.

We all remember best when we are motivated enough to become involved to the degree Katy was.

Attention is selective. It is naturally attracted to items which:

- have strong appeal to the senses—things that are exceptionally colorful, noisy, fragrant, or delicious
- are scary or threatening
- are unusual—weird, shocking, or funny
- compel some kind of action or response
- are thought-provoking—particularly when related to a personal interest

We are naturally alert to and remember anything that deeply concerns us. However, a deliberate effort to focus attention and to concentrate may be necessary to avoid forgetting everyday items—mistakenly heading north when you should be going south or forgetting to take your hostess gift with you. Preventing memory problems like these often depends on being motivated enough to commit to dealing directly with lapses in attention and concentration.

Problems with Attention and Concentration

Interference and distractions create difficulties for attention and concentration.

INTERFERENCE

One item often can interfere with the recall of another. Three factors that contribute to interference are timing, position in a group, and the similarity of items to be recalled.

Timing: The time required to integrate new information into your memory bank depends upon the ease of making one or more connections with what you already know. When events follow each other quite closely, integration of each into your memory bank is difficult or impossible.

Of course, the amount of time required to make a lasting memory trace will be less with familiar material. For instance, if a panel of six representatives from high schools meet to discuss a regional program for teenagers, and the panel members are introduced in rapid-fire succession, out-of-state members of the audience may not register the community and the high school each panel member represents. On the other hand, those in the audience familiar with the region may quickly learn which community and which high school each person represents.

Position in a group: It is usually easier to remember items at the beginning and at the end of a series. These patterns are called the *primacy and recency effects.*

The primacy effect seems to operate because there is the greatest opportunity for review of those items at the beginning. The recency effect occurs because those at the end are still in short term memory until some other information takes their place. Interference is operating when information about the items in the middle has been replaced in your short term memory by newer information.

Interference often takes place when there is no connection made between an item in short term memory and information in long term memory. If, for example, the furniture salesperson is explaining to you the differences in a long row of lounge chairs, you may find that without some sort of connection, no matter how superficial, it is difficult to remember which ones have an extended warranty. Yet, if you note that only the chairs selling over a certain price have this warranty, you'll easily remember if the chair with the style you like best is one of them.

Similarity: The close resemblance of one item or event to another may also cause interference. A hostess who frequently entertains the same friends may not recall which menu she served the last time they came to dinner.

Noticing similarities rather than differences frequently causes interference. In meeting two women of medium height, both of whom are wearing royal blue suits, you might experience interference unless you look for differences in facial contours or hair styles.

Failure to note differences also can occur with some items as complex as screenplays or books. If, within the same week, you saw films based on Jane Austen's books *Pride and Prejudice* and *Sense and Sensibility*, you could become confused about the stories. This is because they are similar in setting, characters, situations, and outcomes. Some modern novelists mass-produce stories with similar characters, settings, and plots. Many fans have difficulty recalling differences among them.

DISTRACTIONS

A second problem concerning our ability to pay attention and concentrate is distractions. Distractions may be external, something in your surroundings, or they may be internal, originating with your own thoughts and feelings.

External Distractions

External distractions are a fact of life. Telephone calls intrude while you're listening to the evening news. The demands of family can be distracting while you're reading the fine print on an insurance policy or figuring out how to operate some new electronic gadget. As a result, you may forget what you have seen or read.

During a bridge game, lively conversation at one table can distract players at other tables. This may cause an expert player to forget how many trumps are still out and go down two doubled and vulnerable—an upsetting event for someone who usually has an excellent memory of which cards have been played.

Even when distractions are created by people you love or things pleasant to hear, they monopolize your attention, break up your concentration, and often fracture your train of thought.

Internal Distractions

Internal distractions are caused by your thoughts or feelings. Making simple connections between some aspect of the present and a piece of your past is a natural thing to do and helps to create a memory. However, concentrating on a past experience may prevent you from focusing on the present.

Dave Hart was doing the marketing. His wife had given him a shopping list and also asked him to post some letters before five o'clock. Dave decided to do the shopping first since the grocery store was on his way to the post office.

One item on the list was sausage. As Dave looked at the different kinds, he was reminded of the smoked sausage his father had ordered every fall from a farmer in New Hampshire. They were thick and brown, and the meat was chunky and seasoned with aromatic herbs. The sausages in the meat case looked unappetizing by comparison.

Dave pushed the buzzer for Joe the butcher to ask if he knew any place to get home-smoked sausages. Joe said, "Funny you should ask. I just heard about a farmer who smokes his own. I'll give you his number."

When Dave telephoned, the farmer said, "Sure, I can let you have some, but you'll have to come today. We're leaving on a trip tomorrow."

Dave agreed to be there in an hour. He thought, I'll finish the shopping and make a quick trip out to the country. We'll have a real treat for breakfast tomorrow.

When he got home, his wife was pleased. She too enjoyed good smoked sausage. However, she also was provoked to discover he had forgotten to mail the letters, one of which was payment for a bill. There would be a sizeable penalty because the check was late.

In this case, making a simple connection of sausage to the smoked sausage of his boyhood evoked Dave's nostalgia and enthusiasm and distracted him from mailing the letters. Worry and frustration also may distract people.

During the first rainstorm of the year, Ruth Ireland's new roof developed a leak over the kitchen. She placed a bucket to catch the drip. When she tried to call the roofer, she found that his phone was busy time and again. She finally reached him and he agreed to come over that evening.

Then her granddaughter's teacher telephoned, "Mrs. Ireland, Suzie said you were going to pick her up. She's been waiting a long time. Aren't you coming?"

Ruth's anxiety about the leak and her inability to reach the plumber were so absorbing that she had forgotten to go for her granddaughter.

We also distract ourselves when we free-associate ideas one after another. This may lead us on tangent after tangent, far from the subject at hand. This is what happened when Natalie Johnson and her friend Judy were planning a program on affirmative action for their club and thinking about possible speakers.

Natalie told Judy that she thought the mayor would be great. "She always reminds me of my Aunt Maggy," Natalie said. "Years ago, she worked hard for women's rights. She visited factories and wrote newspaper articles about the working conditions of women in the garment trade in New York."

"Really?" Judy asked.

"Oh, yes. She was my favorite person as I was growing up. Not everyone liked her though."

"Why not?"

"She was a little too unconventional. My father, who was a minister, really disapproved of her. But I did notice that sometimes he chuckled behind his hand at some of the things she said. She had a great knack for telling stories," Natalie said, lost in her reminiscences.

"I've never been able to do that. I always forget the punch line."

"Me too," Judy said. "I envy people who aren't afraid—"

"Gosh I've forgotten what we were talking about. . . Oh, of course, it was who we might get to speak on affirmative action. . ."

It helps to become aware of such tangents as they develop so you can decide whether proceeding in the new direction seems appropriate. Natalie worked to improve her ability to remain on track by asking herself, "Do I really want to continue with this now?"

We also distract ourselves by planning for the future in the midst of an activity. As a result, we often miss what's happening in the present.

Bob Klose was listening to the evening news which described the President's plan for the budget. Bob started planning what he would include in his letter to the President to criticize that policy. As a result, he didn't hear much of the rest of the broadcast and missed learning about a new regulation which would affect his income tax return.

Developing Better Attention and Concentration

It is important to realize that many memory lapses are, in fact, attention lapses. Since this is so, how do we focus our attention and concentrate differently so this doesn't happen?

Here are five strategies you can use individually or together to combat this problem.

- Increase your effective use of memory aids.

- Develop better habits of attention and concentration.
- Focus on one thing at a time and set your own pace.
- Be aware of your distracting emotions.
- Be open to new ideas.

INCREASE YOUR EFFECTIVE USE OF MEMORY AIDS

A fast and easy way of helping you avoid problems with attention and concentration is to increase your use of memory aids, which are important tools for preventing interference.

> Eleanor Grafton was getting estimates from two contractors for painting the outside of her house. One had been recommended by a friend, the other by the manager of a local paint store.
>
> Eleanor wanted to have some broken stucco and cracks repaired so the damaged areas would blend into the rest of the house. She decided to ask the people who had made the referrals about each contractor's special skills. Then she realized she had forgotten which man had been recommended by her friend and which by the paint store manager.

To Eleanor, both contractors were similar, and, as we've seen, similarity may cause interference. If Eleanor had made a note about each painter as he was referred to her and attached this note to his estimate, there would have been no interference.

Getting yourself into the habit of making lists and keeping records, two primary memory aids, prevents many kinds of memory problems. Calendar notations of menus served to friends are helpful reminders to a hostess concerned with variety in her recipes. "Go by the post office" added to Dave's shopping list could have reminded him to mail the letter before he drove off to buy smoked sausage. A note on the refrigerator could have reminded Ruth to pick up her granddaughter from school.

DEVELOP NEW HABITS OF ATTENTION AND CONCENTRATION

Making the decision to develop strong habits of attention and concentration is an important part of a memory project. As we've seen, memory lapses often involve routine events, those we tend to treat as automatic. However, many really require a second or two of attention. Without this attention, you might find yourself at the gas station when you intended to go to the drug store. Or you may be looking for your car in the spot where you left it yesterday rather than today.

One good habit is to take time to ask yourself: "What am I up to?" "What do I need to do?" You might decide to use this attention habit:

- at specific times, such as when leaving your house
- at places, such as a street intersection where you have several choices

When leaving home, you might ask yourself, "What do I need to take with me?" "Have I turned off. . . ?" "Have I locked up?"

Another good attention habit is to train yourself to develop an awareness of when a routine is interrupted in order to pick up at that point. Lack of this awareness may have undesirable results.

David Moss has a routine of checking his gas gauge as soon as his car warms up in the morning. He does it every day. Yet recently, after switching on the ignition, he realized he'd forgotten his briefcase. Leaving the engine running, he hurried back to get it. He didn't want to be late for a meeting with a new client. Unfortunately, David didn't complete his usual pattern by checking the gas gauge. He ran out of gas, remembering too late that both his wife and son had used his car the day before.

If David had had a mind-set of being alert to an interrupted routine, he could have thought or said, "gas" as a reminder. Or, if on the road to his meeting, David had thought, "Uh oh, interrupted routine," he could then have checked the gas gauge.

Of course, if David had turned off the engine and taken the keys with him when he went back for his briefcase, his routine would have proceeded as usual.

In addition to these *attention* habits, there are two kinds of *concentration* habits which support a good memory.

The first is to minimize distractions either in your environment or in your thinking. Sometimes a little planning in advance will enable you to select an environment free of distracting clutter and noise. You can prevent inner distractions from impeding your concentration by deliberately setting aside, just for the present, all unfinished business, unsolved problems, and emotions which might get in the way of your concentration.

Use this habit to improve your concentration when you are with other people and should be paying attention to their concerns. Attend with your eyes, ears, mind, and intuition.

A second concentration habit is the practice of appropriately refocusing your concentration whenever you are aware of having been distracted either by something in your surroundings or by an irrelevant thought.

A valuable asset in this endeavor is a lifestyle pattern of limiting your concentration to one area of concern at a time.

Focus on One Thing at a Time and Set Your Own Pace

Many memory problems are the result of paying attention to two or more things at once. Most people can remember when they had to do just that. Juggling demands from jobs and children is a necessary skill for adults with growing families. The process becomes more difficult as you grow older. Developing a mind-set of dealing with one attention-demanding thing at a time is an important part of your program for lifelong memory improvement. This is particularly valuable in unfamiliar situations and when stress is involved.

> John Ott was in Paris on business for a few months and knew enough French to get by with shopping and the mechanics of daily living.
>
> One day, however, when late for a business appointment, he tried to follow directions to an unfamiliar location a few kilometers away.
>
> The stress of being late and his unfamiliarity with the streets combined to make him forget the brief directions he'd been given. He became so confused and upset that he finally parked his car, noted the address so he could find it again, and hailed a cab.

John's distress at having to deal with the unfamiliar when he was in a hurry interfered with his remembering correctly what he had been told. If he had allowed enough time to repeat and visualize the instructions clearly and perhaps had written them down or drawn a map, he could have saved time and cab-fare and retained his composure.

A good practice is to set your own pace. Avoid situations where you will be rushed, and you'll avoid many memory problems.

BE AWARE OF YOUR DISTRACTING EMOTIONS

Emotions generated by any experience reinforce the memory of it, regardless of whether they are pleasant or annoying. John probably remembers well his experience of losing his way in Paris. Developing a habit of giving extra attention to how and what you feel about a person, object, or situation reinforces your memory and adds to your memory skills as well.

Yet, emotions unrelated to the present situation, whether positive or negative, may get in the way of your attention and concentration because they distract you from focusing on what is happening at the moment.

Even joyful excitement can cause people to forget. Feeling in "seventh heaven" because you won the lottery may be so overwhelming you forget about the stop sign on the corner near your house. Later, preparations for a trip around the world to enjoy some of your new wealth may be so engrossing that you forget to stop the mail delivery.

In contrast, a man may be so annoyed, downright angry at the glitches with his new computer software and so discouraged at the inability of the publisher to solve the problem that he writes the same letter to an old friend twice, having forgotten it was already written and mailed.

Boredom is another state of mind which can be particularly damaging to attention and concentration. If a person or an event seems dull and humdrum, your level of personal involvement will be minimal.

> Gretchen Long developed a time chart of an average week in order to find out whether she was spending her time in line with her priorities. She discovered that some of her recreation time with other women was essentially boring.
>
> She and the other women had had much in common when

their children were little. Now that time was past, and she was just not interested in neighborhood gossip and the latest crises in TV soap operas. She realized after being with this group that she seldom remembered much that was said, even when it was important.

The group met for coffee every week, but Gretchen decided to propose they meet for lunch once a month instead. She felt she would then pay more attention to what the others were saying.

You too can benefit from being aware of how you feel. Whether glad, sad, mad, scared, or bored, you can decide how best to respond to your feelings so that they reinforce what you want to remember rather than impair your ability to focus and concentrate.

BE OPEN TO NEW IDEAS

Curiosity about new ideas is an important force for improving your attention and concentration. Recognition of the interesting variety of experiences and lifestyles in our multi-cultural world can lead to a desire to learn more about different attitudes, beliefs, and customs.

If you are open to new ideas, do not feel a need to block out unfamiliar or conflicting points of view, and are not concerned with making judgments or defending a position, more of your conscious mind is available to focus on and process new information.

Occasionally, we all discover that long-held attitudes are shortsighted or just plain wrong. Allowing ourselves a broad degree of acceptance and tolerance when presented with new information fosters fresh ways to look at problems and approach solutions. This flexibility when approaching the issues involved in growing older in our changing world keeps our memory skills active and expands our ability to learn and to solve problems.

In contrast, rigid attitudes and beliefs limit attention and concentration and restrict the freedom to listen and to learn. To function from the position that the old ways are the best is like putting on blinders.

Stereotyping, whether it is in regard to age, sex, race, or status, produces unrealistic views of people and of the world. Such stereotypes block the attention you give to the uniqueness of a person or an event thus affecting your memory.

For example, there is no typical older person. Everyone becomes more individualistic with age. The pursuits of men and women past their sixty-fifth birthday run the whole gamut of human interests. Some stay in long-held, well-paying jobs, while others retire and volunteer their time. Finding that responsibilities such as raising children have been eased, some begin a second career. Many men and women make major contributions to their communities long past the age of seventy, defying all stereotypes of the elderly.

Like the other strategies in this chapter, developing an increased openness involves changing your lifestyle patterns as you deal with everyday activities.

Creating these new habits requires patience, self-discipline, and practice. It also takes time. However, this is an investment well-made. Even minor changes will save you time that you once used to retrieve items mislaid or forgotten and spare you the annoyance and embarrassment of memory lapses. You will also acquire a greater degree of control over your life.

Exercises:
Identify and Address Problems with Focusing

1. As you think back over the memory problems you experienced during the past week, do you believe that any of them were the result of inattention? Which ones?

2. If you experienced interference, was it due to timing, position in a group, or similarity of items? How might you have prevented this problem?

3. Was an external distraction involved in any instance? Could you have prevented or reduced it? If so, what might you have done?

4. How about an internal distraction? Could you have prevented or dealt with this?

5. Reexamine the five strategies for improving attention and concentration (See pages 97–98). In which of these strategies would you like to improve?

6. Select one of them to work on in the coming week. How might you do this?

   After you are satisfied with your progress with this strategy, continue with the others.

SIX

Organize Your Learning and Your Life

"**D**ON'T AGONIZE! ORGANIZE!," the motto of the Older Women's League, is good advice for anyone concerned about memory lapses. Unfortunately, some people do agonize about their ability to remember. A more effective response is to build on the fact that an organized approach to learning new things and remembering what is important makes the job easier. Organizing how you spend your time and arrange your surroundings is the key to preventing many memory problems.

The Power of Organization

Your memory is organized as the result of the orderly way in which your brain and nervous system function. As we have seen, nerve cells and brain centers are specialized, each having its own particular task. Communication among these sensory, thought, feeling, and action centers creates the organization you experience as memory.

To prevent the clutter which would interfere with this process, bits and pieces of unexamined information and passing thoughts disappear from your short term memory to leave space for new material.

Many memory lapses are the direct result of this economy. Items you want to remember are lost because they were not integrated into the organization of your memory bank. This integration depends on how you experience and think about the events of every day. Therefore, strategies which contribute to this process play a critical role in building a better memory.

Expand Your Memory

Here are five excellent strategies for developing lifestyle patterns that will help you expand your memory capability and organize yourself in the pursuit of a better memory.

- Develop a mind-set of curiosity and research.
- Break down a complex learning task into units to be mastered one at a time.
- Explore a familiar interest in depth.
- Use existing knowledge and skills in a new setting.
- Study in a new field.

DEVELOP A MIND-SET OF CURIOSITY AND RESEARCH

A mind-set of curiosity and research is expressed by posing and answering questions involving the who, what, why, where, when, and how of any experience. For instance, at a lecture to discuss the needs of public schools, you might ponder:

Who is speaking? What is his background as an authority on the subject? Is he a parent, school principal, professor of education, a state senator?

What is his message? Is there a valid basis for his conclusions? Does the content of the talk persuade you to act in some way?

Why is the subject appealing? Important? Does it relate to your beliefs about education and the responsibility of residents?

Where is the lecture held and under whose auspices? Does the lecture material relate primarily to some place—here, or somewhere else? Does that affect its relevance to your concerns?

When is the lecture being held? Does this date have any impact on the importance of the message? Is it, for example, a month before school starts, or the night before a school board election?

How does the speaker present the material? Is his style open and flexible, or is it rigid and opinionated? Does he use examples to explain and support his statements? Are there opportunities for questions?

In using this strategy of who, what, why, where, when, and how, you amass memory traces related to many types of information. This multi-faceted awareness in any area of life creates a rich experience with numerous memory traces.

BREAK DOWN A COMPLEX LEARNING TASK
New information is more easily stored in your long term memory when each unit builds upon what has gone before.

For example, using a computer requires a mastery—to one degree or another—of the standard keyboard. The next step is to become familiar with software operations and the use of your printer. Once you gain proficiency in these skills, you can learn to put your home budget on an electronic spreadsheet or to use the Internet.

A deliberate, step-by-step approach is an effective way to build a lasting memory of any complex operation.

EXPLORE A FAMILIAR INTEREST IN DEPTH
Enthusiasm for a subject provides the motivation for in-depth study. This happens naturally as people learn a little and want to know more.

For example, you decide you really enjoy snorkeling but wish to progress to scuba diving because of the new vistas and face-to-face contact with creatures in deep water. To become certified, you must study, undergo supervised practice, and pass a test. Stimulating scuba-diving experiences might in turn motivate you to devote more hours of work and study in order to become a dive master. Or you might become so involved with marine life that you study to become a marine biologist.

There's no telling where the exploration of a familiar interest might lead you.

> Clair Bennett enjoyed designing clothing for herself so she decided to go into the business of creating high-style, upbeat clothes for women with figure problems. She prepared herself by learning more about clothing construction, dressmaking tricks, and fabrics. She studied fashion magazines and devised ways to adapt the latest styles to the needs of her clients.

These in-depth approaches collect a multitude of interrelated memory traces.

USE EXISTING KNOWLEDGE AND SKILLS IN A NEW SETTING

When people are proficient in their fields, they often take their knowledge into unfamiliar areas.

A retired businessman devotes his leisure to helping small non-profit organizations with financial planning through the Service Corps of Retired Executives. Thus he gains a new perspective on the funding process.

A retired pediatrician volunteers to tutor disadvantaged children with learning problems and so finds herself in a position to offer guidance and support to families as well. In this unfamiliar environment, she is challenged to find creative ways of helping people meet their needs.

A Kansas farmer and his wife volunteer farming and homemaking experience for work with the Peace Corps. While doing so, they also expand their insights about people and learn how to apply their skills in a third world culture.

As you employ these four strategies, you are expanding your existing memory networks. The fifth strategy involves exploration in an unfamiliar area.

STUDY IN A NEW FIELD

Young people are often forced to make hard decisions and find they must pass up certain interests or opportunities as they study and plan for future careers. As a result, many people nearing retirement decide to spend time doing something they've always wanted to do but never had the chance to pursue.

A retired social worker moves to an artist colony on the Pacific coast to take classes and paint seascapes. A sociology teacher goes back to school to study astronomy.

Concerned about the problems faced by blind children, a retired surgical nurse spends two years learning braille and then transcribes books so that parents can teach their blind children how to read.

With each of these five strategies, you use your mind in ways which increase your memory power overall.

Whether you wish to escalate your curiosity, explore familiar subjects in breadth and depth, or expand your learning into new arenas, you can program yourself to follow new habits increasing your memory networks.

Of course, when you study in a familiar field, there is already a healthy organization of information into which new bits of data can fit nicely. Complex, unfamiliar ideas will take longer to deposit in your memory bank.

More important than previous experience, however, is your motivation. Enthusiasm and eagerness to master a new project will free up the energy to keep you persevering. The rewards will be better memory skills, new ideas to explore, and meaningful activities to enjoy. All of these improve the quality of daily life as well as your memory.

Organize Your Time

As you find yourself applying these strategies, you may be faced with the problem of finding enough time to pursue your interests, and you may decide to make some changes in how you spend your time.

Memory lapses are often the result of a real or perceived lack of minutes in the day to focus clearly or to concentrate on personal priorities. You may forget important information because you lack the time necessary to integrate it. When this is the case, organizing your time more efficiently will help you to build a better memory.

CREATE A TIME BUDGET
The purpose of creating a time budget is to figure out how to balance the way you spend time with your personal wants and needs. A typical time budget might include:

- self maintenance—personal care, meals, exercise, sleep
- household maintenance—chores, shopping, meal preparation, yard work
- work, paid and/or volunteer
- reading and study
- recreation with family and friends

The following example of a time budget covers a typical week in the life of one 58-year-old woman:

Needs and Wants	Estimated hours	%
Self maintenance	77	45
Household maintenance	14	9
Work	44	26
Reading, study	14	9
Recreation	19	11
Totals	168	100

The process of developing a time budget consists of five steps.

1. Make a list of the ways in which you currently spend your time. Include everything which uses a significant block of time. An example is transportation.

2. Select a typical week. With reference to your calendar and your daily routine, estimate what percentage of the week you spent on each kind of activity.

3. Then consider the following questions:

- Does this pattern reflect my priorities?
- If not, to which areas of my life do I want to devote more time?
- Which areas can I make less time-consuming?
- Are there items I can delegate or drop entirely?
- What steps will I need to take in order to make these changes?

4. Design a time budget showing the changes you plan to make.

5. Evaluate your budget by answering such questions as:

- Am I satisfied with this budget as a lifestyle? If not, what do I need to change?
- Are there other activities I want to include? How might I do that?
- Do I need to find better ways to accommodate what I want to do with what I have to do?

Living within such a budget may suggest ways of economizing in your use of time. For instance, you can listen to home study tapes while walking. You can handle household jobs in bits and pieces sandwiched between other activities. Or you might be able to stretch your financial budget to pay others to help with housecleaning or yard work. Saving time sometimes can be more meaningful than saving money.

Working on a time budget also may suggest setting aside thinking time for review and integration of one experience before moving on to the next. This means taking a moment to ask yourself such questions as, "What is special about this experience, this magazine article?" and "What do I want to remember?"

Doing this will help to store the most meaningful items in your memory bank. Thinking time enables you to more easily refocus your attention on the significant aspects of new situations free of external or internal interference.

In your time budget, set aside thinking time devoted exclusively to such personal items as planning, problem solving, and decision making in order to prevent unresolved issues from intruding inappropriately into other areas of your life. By doing this you can clear the decks of unfinished business that would prevent your being fully present at moments you want to remember.

Taking charge of your thinking in this way can play an important role in improving both your memory in general and your prospective memory in particular.

PREPARE FOR FUTURE RECALL

Prospective memory is remembering something for the future, perhaps a bit of information you'll need when you get to the doctor's office or appointments you've made for tomorrow morning. The simplest kind of prospective memory involves holding a task in short term memory. You do this by giving it your attention until the task is completed. An example would be a telephone number you intend to redial after a few minutes have passed.

Most prospective memory, however, requires using memory tools to make connections in your long term memory and/or memory aids to act as reminders. An effective strategy for building a stronger prospective memory involves using both memory tools and memory aids.

If you are driving an unfamiliar road, planning ahead for the return trip may involve spaced verbal reviews, silent or aloud, of landmarks and turns; mental pictures of the route; and visualizing the landmarks in reverse, making associations between the way you see them from one direction and then how they will appear on your return. If this is a trip with many turns, a sketch or brief notes can be a valuable memory aid.

The effective use of a calendar, preparation for special events, and remembering the names of people you expect to run into are three examples requiring prospective memory.

Make Your Calendar Work for You

A calendar is probably the most widely used memory aid. However, its effectiveness depends on an organized plan.

- Keep the calendar in the same spot so you will never forget where it is. Some people have found an attractive wall calendar to be especially useful as an ongoing reminder since the enjoyment of looking at it reinforces the schedule written on it.
- Check your calendar every morning and again at night.
- Before January 1, enter all family holidays and recurring commitments for the new year. These could include regular monthly meetings and dates for bill-paying.
- List in the square for the first Sunday of each month the tasks to schedule some time during that month. Things such as pruning the roses in January, cleaning the gutters in October, and having regular dental checkups.
- Enter all appointments, scheduled meetings, and due dates immediately. If you are often away from home without your calendar, have a small pocket notebook on which to record each item. Then establish a habit of transferring such notes to your calendar promptly, perhaps when you check your telephone answering machine for messages upon returning home.
- Review your tasks and appointments more than once on busy days. You might repeat the sequence silently or aloud and also visualize the way the day's events appear on your calendar.

Plan for Special Events

Advanced planning prevents memory lapses. An organized approach to a complex event such as a wedding or a community benefit involves creating a "plan of work." This covers the essential tasks and tells when and where they will be held and who will complete them.

Kathy Chang agreed to chair the annual benefit for Meals on Wheels. Checking the minutes of last year's event, she made a list of the tasks involved.

At the first committee meeting there was discussion of the previous party. The attendees developed a plan of work with a time line and the names of the men and women responsible for essential tasks:

- publicity
- decorations
- budget
- requests to restaurants for food donations
- requests to stores for discounts on beverages
- contacts with banks and other businesses for contributions to cover printing, janitorial services, and music
- recruitment of on-site help

Future meetings were scheduled for:

- progress reports
- final plans
- evaluation and letters of appreciation to all contributors

Because this was such a complex event with so many people involved, each person who attended was mailed copies of the plan and the minutes. These memory aids provided insurance against memory lapses.

Another planning strategy involving prospective memory can help you remember men and women and their names.

Plan to Remember People

Some people feel inadequate because they fail to remember names. If you feel this way, before any meeting, take a few minutes of extra thought about whom you will be seeing. If you wish, check the notes you made after a previous meeting or ask a friend or family member to help jog your memory. This is called "priming your memory pump."

If possible, learn in advance the names of strangers you'll be meeting and bits of information about them. This creates memory traces that are built upon when the meeting does take place and helps you to recall names and other details when needed.

Priming the pump works with longtime friends too. This consists of bringing old memories to the surface to have them readily available for recall. Spend a little time before meeting old friends to think about previous visits, events, and concerns in their lives.

You might recall an amusing incident you shared during a golf game, the name of your friend's new grandchild, or the great joke the two of you heard from the waiter at your favorite restaurant. Such items can stimulate your memory and liven up your time together.

Priming the memory pump can be useful in helping you recall experiences from the distant past. An impending class reunion offers an opportunity for organizing yourself to remember people and their names. Going through an old yearbook will call to mind memories of activities shared with friends, experiences you then can easily recall at the reunion. Discussing these activities with the other alumni at the event will lead to additional shared memories.

Thinking ahead in order to be prepared is the essential factor in these examples. In addition, you can prepare yourself to remember all these experiences by planning to give both the people and the events you share your full attention.

Prepare for Emergencies

Critical problems with forgetting often occur during the stress of an emergency. Time spent in preparing for a possible crisis is time well spent.

Many people in earthquake country store the necessities to enable them and their families to survive for a crucial period. They use checklists of these necessary items and notes of the dates that water and foodstuff need to be replaced as memory aids.

Planning for personal emergencies such as the unexpected onset of a severe illness is important.

Recognizing that in emergencies people do forget things provides the motivation to do such advanced planning. Responding to the question, "What would I do if. . . ?" leads to the preparations enabling you to remember the important things.

Pamphlets available from the Red Cross provide guidelines to organize your household for such crises.

Organize Your Surroundings

Have you ever had the experience of searching frantically for an important paper and then, in desperation, returning to the appropriate file to find it was there all the time? Perhaps the folder is crowded with papers which could have been sorted and weeded out long ago.

In a cluttered or crowded environment, misplaced items often defy detection. Organizing your surroundings can abolish distracting clutter and prevent many common memory lapses, such as forgetting where you put your birth certificate, bank statement, or the dill weed for your favorite sauce recipe.

If you are to deal comfortably with the demands of modern life, having a well-organized place in which to function is vital. Organizing your home is an important step in building a better memory.

Many books are available with instructions on organizing your household, from linen closets to kitchen cupboards and from file cabinets to work benches. Here are some of the things you can do to abolish clutter in support of a better memory:

- Remove from your immediate environment items which you don't use. Store or dispose of the papers, clothing, or kitchen tools you will not be needing in the foreseeable future.
- Adopt logical plans. These may involve assigning space in closets and cupboards and using a filing system for papers. You might create an inventory for your important possessions and an index for the filing system. A list of the contents on the face of each file drawer is a timesaving memory aid.
- Have a place for everything. This includes keys, eyeglasses, paid and unpaid bills, checkbooks, insurance papers, tax records, certificates, and great grandmother's Tiffany watch, all of which are easily misplaced.
- Keep everything in its place. Committing yourself to this degree of organization will bring you personal satisfaction and prevent many anguished moments. If you always put every item where it belongs, you won't have to remember where you left it. Frantic searches will be at an end, or at least kept to a minimum.
- Develop a procedure for handling mail. This, for many people, creates the greatest clutter of anything in the house. Develop a system that works for you, then always be sure to use it.
- Create a file of important papers. This should contain any information needed in an emergency if you were unavailable. These would include your bankbook, a list of assets, insurance papers, a list of the location and inventory of your safety deposit box, a copy of

your will, and names of people such as your lawyer or doctor. In the event of a crisis, those who care about you will appreciate such an organized approach. The added value is that without hesitation you will be able to recall the location of these important papers.

Any way you can bring greater order into your environment will keep distractions at a minimum and support good memory functioning. This organization will also free up time and energy which you can use to focus on projects that interest you.

Exercises:
Plan Your Organization

1. Review the strategies for developing lifestyle patterns that will help you expand your memory capability and organize yourself. (See page 107.) Are you currently using any of them?

2. Which of these strategies might you use in working toward your goals? In what context?

3. How do you feel about your use of time?

    Never enough?

    About right?

    Time on your hands?

    If you are not satisfied, what steps can you take to improve your use of time?

4. Make up what you would consider an ideal time budget in your present situation. How might you move your current ways of spending time closer to that ideal?

5. Is there something you want to do that you seem never to have enough time for? Can you build this into your time budget? If so, how?

6. Rate the organization of your surroundings from one to ten with one being poor and ten being superior. If you are not satisfied with your self-rating, in what areas can you create more organization with an eye to preventing memory lapses in the future?

SEVEN

Take Care
of Your Health

Have you ever noticed that when you're overtired or under the weather, you forget even the simplest things?

Your brain is so delicately attuned to the rest of your body that it may be affected by a discomfort or malfunction in any body system. Taking care of your health—physical, mental, and emotional—is a vital part of any effective memory improvement program. Five disciplines figure into a healthy lifestyle and in turn, a healthy memory:

- a nutritious diet
- regular physical and mental exercise
- limiting exposure to toxins
- avoiding or limiting medications affecting memory
- regular medical checkups to permit early diagnosis and treatment of health problems

Eat Your Way to a Better Memory

Brain cells are particularly sensitive to the quality of your diet. Since the body does not maintain a reserve of some nutrients, adopting a well balanced diet is an important part of a health maintenance program.

The results of solid research on nutrition are shown in the U. S.

Department of Agriculture Food Guide Pyramid. The base of the pyramid represents the six to eleven daily servings of bread, cereal, rice, and pasta suggested as part of a healthy diet. The next level represents the suggested three to five servings of vegetables and two to four servings of fruit. Above this is a group of two to three servings of milk, yogurt, and cheese and two to three servings of meat, poultry, fish, dry beans, eggs, and nuts. At the peak of the pyramid are fats, oils, and sweets, which are to be eaten only sparingly.

This diet supports the health of the whole body and is the basis for a well-functioning brain and nervous system which depend on vitamins, minerals and other nutrients from our diet. Using the pyramid as a guide helps ensure the inclusion and the correct balance of the essentials.

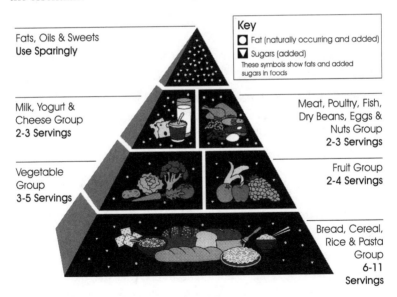

U.S.D.A. Food Guide Pyramid

B Vitamins and Memory

The B vitamins seem especially critical to thought and memory. Research on memory tasks has shown that healthy older adults score poorly when they have low blood levels of B vitamins. Vitamins B6, B12, and folic acid (a B vitamin) have been shown to be directly related to memory functioning.

- B6 is found in meat, poultry, fish, green leafy vegetables, whole grains and cereals, soy beans, nuts, sweet potatoes, and bananas.
- Vitamin B12 is found in meat, eggs, fish, and dairy products.
- Folic acid is found in citrus fruit, green leafy vegetables, legumes, dried beans, and brewer's yeast.

A drop in the secretion of stomach acid as people grow older may hinder the absorption of B12, and this may cause forgetfulness in old age. Also a strictly vegetarian diet does not contain adequate B12. A medical test can identify this deficiency, which can be treated successfully.

In addition to feeding cells, a healthy diet helps to protect them from damage by free radicals.

Free Radicals, Antioxidants, and Memory

Free radicals are unstable oxygen molecules which occur naturally as waste products of metabolism. They form inside and between cells when oxygen reacts with fat in the diet. This oxidation, like rust on metal, damages the cell and cell membrane. Other free radicals which damage cells result from contaminants such as agricultural sprays on food, smoke, other fumes in the air, and chemicals in drinking water.

A free radical is an unstable molecule because it is seeking a missing electron and does its damage by taking electrons from stable molecules and turning them into more free radicals. The body has some natural defenses against free radicals, but these are limited and seem to be less effective as people grow older.

An antioxidant is a natural chemical in food which supplies the missing electron. Thus antioxidants inhibit oxidation and are natural scavengers which help to protect cells from free radicals.

National Academy of Science research on gerbils has shown that damage by free radicals causes memory loss and that antioxidants restore it. The experimentation shows that continued treatment with antioxidants was necessary in order to maintain the memory improvement in the gerbils. This research emphasizes the importance of antioxidants as part of a regular diet and suggests the possibility that antioxidants might reverse the damage to memory caused by free radicals in humans.

Antioxidants include vitamins, minerals, and other chemicals found only in fruits and vegetables, whole grains, legumes, nuts, and seeds. Vitamins C, E, and beta carotene seem to be the major antioxidants, and to work best together.

- Vitamin C is found in citrus fruits, tomatoes, cantaloupe, strawberries, papaya, kiwi fruit, broccoli, brussels sprouts, and peppers.
- Vitamin E is found in whole grains, wheat germ, nuts, seeds, and corn, sunflower, and soybean oils.
- Beta carotene is contained in yellow and orange fruits and vegetables and in green leafy vegetables.

Other antioxidants include selenium—found in grains, cereals, rice, and pasta—and ingredients in berries, garlic, tomatoes, and in green and black tea.

The primary source of antioxidants should be food rather than supplements since supplements do not contain other valuable nutrients. However, a daily vitamin and mineral supplement is recommended by many researchers to compensate for deficits. The American Medical Association states that a one-a-day supplement should not exceed the Recommended Daily Allowance, the R. D. A. , as determined by the Food and Nutrition Board of the National Academy of Sciences. This supplement should include iron only with a doctor's recommendation since an excess of iron fosters damage from free radicals.

Concern about staying healthy has generated a growing market in food supplements, many of which are not regulated by any government agency. Taking a "miracle food" supplement on the basis of stories of remarkable results may not constitute your best investment and could damage your health. Consult your health-care professional for advice.

Research in nutrition is ongoing, and staying informed about new discoveries is an important part of staying healthy. Excellent resources for this are the health newsletters published by universities and articles and books written by reputable professionals which are based on solid research and scientific testing rather than on anecdotal accounts.

Circulation and Your Memory

An effective cardiovascular system ensures that nutrients are transported to the cells. Because of this, maintaining the health of this system is critical to a good memory. Antioxidants seem to contribute to the flexibility of blood vessel walls by helping to prevent the formation of arterial plaques which block blood flow.

Cholesterol plays a critical role in the creation of these plaques. Cholesterol is a waxy substance produced by the liver. It also enters our body through animal products we eat. Cholesterol is essential in forming vital hormones and metabolic products, but too much cholesterol is a problem. Since the human body seems to produce enough cholesterol for its needs, eating foods high in cholesterol is thought to be unwarranted.

There are two types of cholesterol:

- "Bad" (LDL, or low density lipoprotein) cholesterol deposits on the arterial walls contributing to the buildup of plaque.
- "Good" (HDL, or high density lipoprotein) cholesterol actually draws bad cholesterol away from the linings of the arteries. Good cholesterol levels seem to increase with a diet rich in antioxidants.

The health of the circulatory system involves the prevention or reversal of plaque-blocked blood vessels. Two types of edible fats have a major impact on levels of cholesterol in our blood. They are saturated and unsaturated fats.

Saturated fats raise the level of harmful cholesterol and are found in meat, butter, cheese, whole milk, palm, coconut, and hydrogenated oils.

There are two types of unsaturated fats, polyunsaturated and monounsaturated. Polyunsaturated fats lower levels of both good and bad cholesterol. They are found in corn, safflower, and sunflower seed oils. Monounsaturated fats lower the bad cholesterol only. These are found in olive and canola oils.

A low-fat, low-cholesterol diet helps keep blood vessels open. Dietary guidelines supporting a healthy cardiovascular system focus on:

- reduction of saturated fats in favor of unsaturated fats, particularly the monounsaturates
- reduction of the intake of cholesterol, which is found in meat, butter, eggs, milk, and other animal products

Cholesterol does not exist in plant foods, and a regimen which includes a vegetarian diet supervised by a medical professional has proved healthy for people with severe cholesterol problems.

Some nutritional problems result from a changing social environment as people grow older. Men and women living alone often get bored with food preparation. The temptation for someone eating alone day after day is to do the easy thing, which may not be the healthy thing. Many men living alone seem to be particularly at risk for inadequate nutrition.

Changing lifelong patterns of nutrition may seem difficult, but often small dietary changes can make a significant difference in health and well-being.

Developing a plan to ensure nutritious and pleasant meals will pay big dividends in terms of both health and personal enjoyment. Such a plan might involve exchanging meals with friends, organizing a Chat and Chew Club, or attending a congregate luncheon site. Combining lectures or classes with a meal program would provide food for both mind and body.

Physical Exercise and Memory

Studies in aging and memory have demonstrated that exercise supports a good memory. Healthy people in their seventies participating in a program of regular physical activity have been compared with equally healthy people of the same age living a sedentary lifestyle. The men and women with the exercise program tested significantly better in both thinking and memory skills.

The circulatory system receives many benefits from exercise. It raises the level of good cholesterol and builds up smaller blood vessels to reduce the load on the arteries. It increases the efficiency of the heart in pumping nutrients and oxygen to nerve cells. It expands breathing capacity and strengthens the muscles that control expansion and contraction of the lungs. This affects the supply of oxygen available to meet the needs of cells.

Exercise also lowers blood pressure. Memory problems often accompany high blood pressure, and high blood pressure in middle age has been found to predict poorer memory and thinking skills twenty years in the future.

Physically active people seem to have more elasticity in their arteries than those with a sedentary lifestyle, and reduced elasticity relates directly to high blood pressure. It squeezes the blood flow and hastens the buildup of fats and other substances inside the arteries. As the lining of arteries stiffens and loses flexibility, blood moves through them with increasing difficulty. With chronic high blood pressure, the heart is working continuously against increased pressure from the arteries.

Exercise also raises the metabolic rate at which calories are burned. The increased rate, which may continue for as much as six hours after an exercise period, helps rid the body of excess weight. Since being overweight predisposes people to high blood pressure, keeping body weight within normal limits through a healthy diet and regular exercise is an important element in a memory program.

Exercise need not be strenuous or expensive like playing tennis or working out at a health club. Activities like walking, bicycling, and swimming can increase heart and breathing rates, lower blood pressure, raise good cholesterol levels, and regulate weight. A program approved by your health care professional consisting of an exercise plan and a diet low in salt, fats, and sugars is an ideal approach to the all-too-common problem of being overweight.

EXERCISE AND NERVE CELL GROWTH

An additional benefit of exercise is that it increases neuron growth factors. These are biochemicals which:

- promote new growth on nerve cells
- protect them from oxidation damage
- contribute to the long term maintenance of your nervous system

Neuron growth factors are affected by the amount of activity at a synapse, the gap between cells. The connections across these gaps allow information to pass to other cells in the communication network.

As you exercise, stimulation of one neuron by another increases the production of growth factors, which then react on these neurons and upon other neurons as well. Therefore, physical exercise is an important aspect of a memory project.

Mental Exercise and Memory

If exercising brain power were as common a discipline as keeping physically fit, then a lot fewer people would be complaining about memory lapses. The great importance of mental stimulation for a healthy memory has been demonstrated by the experience of people with sharp minds and good memories in their eighties and nineties, as well as by research. Probably everyone reading this book has either known or known of a very elderly person who is "sharp as a tack."

Eighty-two-year-old Hilda Peterson had had a very busy volunteer and social life since her husband's death. She was active in her church and tutored delinquent boys at the Boys' Farm. In getting out of her car one day, she fell and fractured her hip. In that moment her whole life changed.

Her convalescence threatened to be a long one, and, since she often wondered what life was like for her ancestors in France and Germany, she decided to devote time to studying European history.

A friend who dropped in to call asked, "Hilda, why on earth are you spending all that time on something you can't ever use?"

She responded, "Because it's fascinating." She went on to say that perhaps breaking her hip was a blessing in disguise. "All this reading has added a whole new dimension to my life," she told her friend.

Not only is studying a subject she's interested in helping to make Hilda's convalescence less boring, but she is stimulating her brain cells and memory.

However, improving your memory skills need not be all study and little play. Many games exercise working memory by creating challenges that employ, exercise, and expand thinking skills.

Bridge is a fine example. You don't have to excel at duplicate or win tournaments for your memory to benefit from the game. A novice, in particular, will be expanding memory ability. Working memory calls on the rules of the game stored in long term memory, totals the point count value of a hand, debates possible bids, and then correlates them with bids of other players and their personal style of play.

From the first lead, the bridge player is continuously watching the cards played, counting, and guessing where the trumps and high cards lie. Bidding and making a bridge contract require memory skills and uncluttered attention and concentration. In addition, reviewing the game, sometimes play by play, calls on recent long term memory.

Chess exercises thinking skills including spatial memory. Even a beginner is constantly comparing, estimating, mentally testing moves, and trying to predict an opponent's next move. Chess makes significant demands on both working and long term memory when the present situation is compared with past experience. During a game, skilled players often mentally review famous games while trying to predict which strategy an opponent will use.

Many kinds of play which improve memory but do not require more than one person are available. There is a big variety of electronic games. Crossword puzzles, acrostics, and other word puzzles are excellent tools for exercising your working memory and for expanding your active vocabulary.

Physical sports have aspects which work to support your memory power. The intense concentration on a golf swing or tennis stroke contributes to your memory skills. Committed athletes continually work on improving their techniques and also are sensitive to their performances and that of others in competitions.

Spectators who are devoted fans may think and talk baseball, football, basketball, or hockey to the exclusion of much else during the season. They observe, compare and contrast, comb the sports page for information, and often are so motivated that they remember even the tiniest bit of trivia connected with the sport. Their passion ensures that their memory skills are well exercised.

As opposed to the spectator rats described in Chapter One—

those that showed no growth of brain cells because they were uninvolved—fans of team sports are actively working with what they see, hear, read, and learn. Such activity calls on the resources of working memory and both recent and remote long term memory. All of this, of course, is reinforced by pleasure in the game.

Building mental exercise into your lifestyle is a major step toward improving your memory. This involves adopting a mind-set of commitment to lifelong learning through asking, listening, reading, and study. You might be curious about ethnic diets and recipes, computers and the Internet, Eastern religions, modern art, or new physics—anything that grabs your attention. The resources for mental exercise are endless, and they all contribute to the kinds of challenges which grow branches on nerve cells.

Limit Your Exposure to Toxins

An important way of maintaining the health of your brain is to become aware of toxins in your environment and to use appropriate safeguards to protect yourself. Water contamination is usually brought promptly to the attention of the public, but there often is no easy way we can learn whether the fish we eat comes from polluted water or if our poultry has been treated with additives. Chemicals used on food include pesticides, fungicides, and fertilizers. There is, as yet, much we do not know about the long term effects of many of these chemicals. People respond to this uncertainty in their own ways. Some scrub and peel all produce to remove sprays. Others raise their own fruits and vegetables and become vegetarians. Still others buy organic produce, milk and meat grown without hormones, and bottled water. Reading product labels and asking your grocer or butcher about specific products will help keep you informed about food safety.

Many commonly used chemicals are toxic. They include gasoline, household cleaning products, and aerosol sprays. The damage by tobacco smoke to lungs and the cardiovascular system has been well documented.

Alcohol is a chemical that is a mixed blessing for memory. A little of it increases good cholesterol. However, memory functioning is adversely affected by greater amounts, as anyone who has experienced a severe hangover can testify. Chronic abuse of alcohol reduces the store and interferes with the absorption of the B Vitamins. Alcohol can damage or destroy brain cells.

Limiting your intake and avoiding chronic use makes for a healthy body and brain.

The U. S. Department of Health and Human Services identifies moderate alcohol consumption as one drink a day for women and two for men. A drink is:

- 12 oz. of regular beer
- 1.5 oz. of 80-proof distilled spirits
- 4 to 5 oz. of wine

UNDERSTAND YOUR MEDICATION

Many medications have side effects that affect memory. These include some antihistamines, antispasmodics, and sleeping pills, as well as medications for pain, arthritis, colds, coughs, anxiety, depression, high blood pressure, and heart disease. Also included are some drugs that suppress stomach acid.

Discussing the action and side effects of your medications with your doctor is an important part of safeguarding your memory. In some cases, reducing the dosage or substituting another medication—under your doctor's supervision—may prevent side effects.

Drugs taken in combination may have side effects. If you are seeing several doctors, inform each about all of your medications.

Your pharmacist is an excellent source of information about drugs or combinations of drugs and also about the interactions of prescription medications with over-the-counter drugs. Always ask about side effects, interactions with other medications, and what to do if you miss a dose. Consistent use of the same pharmacist can provide expert supervision of your medication patterns and also will mean that all your records are in one location.

Keep in Touch with Your Doctor

Regular medical checkups are an important part of any health maintenance program. If you are having persistent memory problems, talk to your physician about them.

It may be just a misperception by you or those around you that you're not remembering as well as you used to, but recent, persistent memory problems could be a symptom of a cardiovascular condition, diabetes, thyroid dysfunction, or a lung, liver, or kidney problem, as well as a side effect from a drug. Often such conditions can be reversed or controlled by medical procedures. Treating the medical problem frequently will solve the memory problem.

In any case, discussing memory problems with your doctor is an important part of taking charge of your health.

Alzheimer's Disease

Alzheimer's is not an aspect of normal aging. It is a progressive disease in which memory loss is the primary symptom.

In very early stages a person seems to need more memory traces in order to recall information. Later there are more severe types of memory loss such as:

- getting lost in familiar territory
- difficulty in recalling common words
- forgetting the names or relationships of family members and friends
- becoming disoriented as to time and place
- repeating the same information over and over to the same person
- inability to manage tasks that were previously routine

Additional symptoms are changes in mood and personality and loss of judgment and motivation. Typically, family and friends are more worried about such changes than the patient himself.

Extensive research has failed to identify the cause or causes of the disease, although some cases seem to have a genetic component. Current goals of research are to identify factors which protect against the disease and to develop ways of extending a good quality of life for those in the early stages.

Diagnosis of Alzheimer's disease in its early stages is important because there are now several medications prescribed for this period which, in some cases, slow down the progress of the disease.

Nonsteroid anti-inflammatory drugs, estrogen replacement medication, and vitamin E may offer some protection against the disease. However, firm evidence concerning effective or safe dosages and possible side effects is still not available. A doctor should be consulted in determining what is appropriate for any particular person.

Education also seems to be a protective factor, possibly as a result of having a greater number of dendrite branches and synapses in reserve to fill in for those lost or damaged by the disease. The value of lifelong education for everyone, regardless of age or state of health, is, of course, a major theme of this book.

Many communities have developed activity programs serving people in early or moderate stages of Alzheimer's. Support groups for care-givers provide up-to-date information about resources and useful techniques for care-giving as well as mutual support. Respite programs have been helpful for care-givers who need a few hours or days of freedom from their responsibilities.

Exercises:
Evaluate Your Lifestyle for Health Concerns

1. Review the elements of a sound health maintenance program. (See page 122.) Are there any that you currently are neglecting? If so, what action might you take?
2. Does your lifestyle include:

   • physical activities just for fun?
   • mental activities just for fun?

3. If there are changes you would like to make, write an action plan including what you expect to do and when.

EIGHT

Deal with Stress and Depression

IN OUR MODERN SOCIETY, stress has gotten bad press. Yet low-level stress can be an asset if it mobilizes energy in response to challenging events of your life.

One way healthy levels of stress contribute to personal growth is by creating opportunities for learning. For instance, mastering the use of a computer takes patience and perseverance. It is often stressful. Yet, in spite of problems and mistakes, many find the challenge irresistible, with each success exhilarating.

Stress becomes distress when you feel overwhelmed and unable to cope with a difficult situation. Suppose you've just begun to feel competent and delighted with your new computer. You've discovered it's both a tool and a toy. Then one day, as you're working against a deadline, the computer locks up and you lose an hour's work. Surely you must have hit the wrong key. When this happens a second and a third time, you telephone your consultant for help. A recorded message says he is on vacation for two weeks.

At this point your stress level may soar. You have a clear choice: take positive action to deal with the problem or feel overwhelmed.

You decide on positive action and a short time later, to your great relief, you locate another consultant who solves the problem. You learn what you did wrong and how timed backups will eliminate such catastrophes. You continue with your work, feeling self-confident and in control.

Maintaining a positive attitude and not giving in to stress frees you to keep expanding your memory skills and makes life more pleasant. Optimists use hope, courage, self-acceptance, and past experience when confronting the challenges of their lives. When they feel a need for more, they look for new resources, brainstorm with friends, or seek professional help. Staying in a positive frame of mind alleviates stress and frees energy for memory duty.

Physical Impact of Stress on Memory

Stress is a physical response to a threat, real or imagined. Stress helps us to marshal our energies to meet the challenges of daily living. When threatened, the body mobilizes itself to use all of its resources to fight or flee. The result is heightened muscle tension, and increases in blood pressure, rate of breathing, and metabolism to help provide the necessary energy. In order to free additional energy, the supportive services of digestion, growth and repair, immune system functioning, and reproduction are cut back. These changes are accompanied by an increase in mental alertness. All of this prepares an individual to respond to the crisis.

When the crisis ends, these supportive systems begin to return to normal. Yet continuing stress, such as occurs with an ongoing financial problem, depletes your energy. And the stress-related loss of critical immune system defenses and healing powers leaves your body at risk. Stress-induced high blood pressure increases the possibility of cardiovascular disease.

The physical impact of stress on memory has been revealed in more than fifteen years of research with baboons on the Serengeti Plain in Tanganyika. This study by Robert Sapolsky, author of *Why Zebras Don't Get Ulcers: A Guide to Stress, Stress Related Diseases, and*

Coping, shows that excessive stress damages, or makes more susceptible to damage, the nerve cells in the parts of the brain which sort and organize new information for storage in long term memory. The importance of this cannot be overestimated. While such brain research with human beings presents difficulties, recognizing the danger of similar damage for us is appropriate.

Stress dilutes the attention essential to memory because it focuses on a real or imagined threat. The result is like putting on blinders. If the stress continues, fatigue sets in. Concentration and organized thinking become fragmented.

Life Experiences and Stress

Threats to our physical well-being have changed since the early days of man. In our world, wild beasts have been replaced by crime and war. Drug wars in our communities and children settling their arguments with guns occur all too frequently. During these tragedies and their aftermath, it is, of course, common to suffer acute and chronic stress.

However, much present-day stress is the response to mental discomforts or forebodings rather than impending physical attack. Some of this stress is caused by changing financial situations, worry about the health and well-being of yourself or loved ones, and all the little things that can and do go wrong in a modern household.

Having worked through mid-life issues involving jobs and family, many men and women look forward to the special gifts of retirement. Additional leisure time, travel, return to school, work with the arts, or volunteering in the community all bring new challenges creating the healthy stress that keeps people young at heart. This keeps memory skills exercised, honed, and expanded. This is indeed a time to enjoy living.

However, for most people, the last third of their lives brings negative experiences that range from mildly stressful to very stressful. Health changes may interfere with pursuing favorite sports or hobbies. Financial problems may become overwhelming if retirement income does not keep pace with inflation. Unexpected medical expenses can deplete reserves.

Social problems create stress. Loss of a prized job or a leadership role in the community can rob someone of an important part of his sense of identity. Other social issues include loss of a spouse through divorce or death. These events sometimes separate people who have spent the majority of their lives together. In addition to the loneliness and grief, these changes mean loss of the role of being a member of a couple, the social unit for much leisure-time activity.

Unfortunately, as the years go by, the process of returning to physical equilibrium after resolution of stress takes longer. Sometimes there are no perfect solutions and hard choices between undesirable alternatives may be necessary. In some cases, the imbalance may last indefinitely.

People who are able to address with hope and self-confidence the life changes they experience are best able to maintain their physical health and their memory skills as well. Developing a lifestyle of coping positively and creatively with the stresses that do occur is an important task.

Strategies for Minimizing Stress

Robert Sapolsky has identified four factors that contribute to successful strategies for dealing with stress:

- control
- predictability of the outcome

- social supports
- an outlet for feelings

These factors apply differently in each situation, and we all apply them in unique ways. But a positive, hopeful approach to stressful situations and acceptance of situations which cannot be changed will help you to cope.

CONTROL

The sense of having any amount of control, even the illusion of control, is significant in reducing the physical impact of stress.

Research in nursing homes has shown that the stress level of residents is reduced when they are given some choices over such things as mealtimes, foods, and clothing.

The opportunity to have such control is effective in reducing stress even if people do not take advantage of it.

In confronting stress, an important task is to determine the degree of control you can exert over the situation causing the stress. The realization that some control is possible brings an openness to explore all available options. Brainstorming with friends or consulting a member of the clergy, social worker, or counselor can further expand options and help you make the best decisions possible.

There are, of course, events over which you typically have little or no control, such as past actions or irretrievable losses. Yet, things done or left undone, or words said or not said, can often be atoned for in real or symbolic ways. In many cases, adopting a new attitude helps you to move on with meaningful living.

People deal with grief in their own time. The denial, the sadness, the anger, and the feelings of loneliness take time to work through. The varied ways of coping with such losses are beyond the scope of this book, but a number of helpful books are included in the bibliography.

There are very few situations over which you have absolutely no control. Brainstorming your options enables you to make your own decisions.

Centering is a way of increasing the experience of being in control. This is a technique for inducing a sense of inner serenity in which the body moves toward the ideal physical and biochemical balance bringing about an absence of stress. The regular practice of centering can induce this state of deep relaxation.

Meditation is one method of reaching this balance. Ways of meditating have evolved in many cultures over the centuries. Branches of the major religions have developed their own patterns of inducing a sense of inner peace and unity.

Herbert Benson, author of *The Relaxation Response*, suggests four elements for effective meditation:

- a quiet environment, which may be either inside or outdoors
- an item to focus upon, such as an object, a word, phrase, or a sound
- a passive attitude
- a comfortable position

Avoid lying down, however. It may cause you to slip from meditation into sleep.

Western medical research has shown that Transcendental Meditation, which originated in Asia, reduces the physical and biochemical factors making up the stress response.

TM reduces heart and breathing rates and increases the intensity and frequency of the brain waves which accompany a sense of well-being and serenity.

Tests showed it also reduced high blood pressure. The lowered pressure continued unless the person stopped practicing periodic meditation. (Medical supervision is essential for anyone taking blood pressure medication and beginning meditation.)

In TM, you sit at rest, eyes closed, in a straight chair, in a quiet room with no bright lights or distractions. You repeat silently a mantra consisting of a single word or a phrase. The purpose is to silence other thoughts, feelings, or sensations which are allowed to "drift away like autumn leaves." You meditate for twenty minutes twice a day, before breakfast and before the evening meal.

Men and women who practice TM report a deep sense of peace and wholeness and an increase in energy. This allows them to focus their attention on whatever seems important, the ideal state for creating memories.

This calm, energized condition is in direct contrast to feeling worried by the enormity of a situation, scattered by conflicting thoughts, or distracted by varying demands for attention, all of which interfere with memory functioning.

Some other ways of centering are:

- deep breathing exercises, where the focus is on the breathing process
- progressive relaxation, from your toes to your head, sometimes followed by a fantasy trip to a safe and beautiful place where you feel at peace
- body movement patterns such as yoga or tai chi

Regular practice of any centering technique is necessary to continue progressing toward a deeply relaxed state. The more weeks, months, and years, you practice, the more effective you will be in inducing a state of relaxation.

PREDICTABILITY

Stress reduction clearly contributes to a sense of being in control of your life. It supports clear thinking for solving problems and making decisions about how to deal with stressful situations.

A major concern in such decision-making is the question of predictability: Can the probable outcome be predicted?

The desire for predictability varies from person to person and situation to situation. To know the probable outcome reduces the possibility of surprise, which in itself is stressful. Yet some people seem to deny as long as possible any news that threatens their lifestyle.

With traumatic predictions, such as a critical illness, people may need time to adapt their thinking to an unexpected and unwelcome future. The first response may be denial, "It's just not possible." However, keeping a great worry bottled up indefinitely requires a lot of energy and adds to stress.

In a painful situation, you can often take control over what you learn and how your learn it. Ask for information in manageable bits to permit yourself the time necessary to work through and assimilate it. Or you may want to get the news—no matter how upsetting—all at once. In the last analysis, having information, whether early or late, enables you to plan for the future.

Confronting and dealing with a prediction often means the present can be identified as precious and meaningful, to be enjoyed moment by moment.

SOCIAL SUPPORTS

Social supports are a major asset in coping with stress. Just being able to share and feel understood can be extremely helpful when you are worried, anxious, or grieving. In the process, you can often acquire a new perspective about the situation causing the concern.

The need for social support also is an area in which people differ. We choose what we think will work for us. Sometimes we want to be alone to work through problems. At other times, we may feel relief and gain insight from sharing with a friend.

Support groups, formal or informal, allow you to share while giving support to and gaining support from others with similar concerns. Grief support groups are sponsored by the American Association of Retired Persons and many houses of worship in response to the problems created by bereavement. Such organizations as Experience Unlimited have groups to help people deal with late-in-a-career unemployment. Parents Without Partners and some parent-teachers associations help single adults, including grandparents, with the stressful tasks of raising children alone.

A number of groups address problems created by alcohol abuse, a major cause of memory problems:

- Alcoholics Anonymous for people addicted to alcohol
- Alanon for family members of alcoholics
- Alateen for teenagers

There are similar programs addressing addiction to drugs, sex, and gambling.

Many hospitals have support groups for seriously ill patients. Caregivers and family members may meet separately at the same time. Such activities are designed to meet the needs of everyone involved.

OUTLETS

Having an outlet for the emotional energy associated with stress is an important aid in coping with life's more difficult challenges.

Molly Martinez' husband Ken had Alzheimer's disease. She dealt with her frustration and despair about their lost dreams and plans for retirement by writing poetry, some of which focused on their marriage and her feelings about their past life together. In others, she described experiences of some of the people in Asian countries where she and Ken had lived.

Before she started to write, she often visualized the experience she wanted to describe, letting her memory take her into another place and time. Then she let the words flow from that memory. In this other world, she forgot the sadness of her days and her worries about the future.

Reexperiencing those meaningful moments worked as an outlet and gave her the strength and courage to make the hard decision to move Ken into a protected setting as recommended by his physician.

In the lives of most of us, all four of the factors identified by Sapolsky work together to help us cope with stress. This is the case with Lillian Norton.

Lillian sat in her study. It was almost a year since her husband Frank had died of a heart attack. This would have been their wedding anniversary, and she was recalling memories of other anniversaries and events of their life together.

She felt she'd never stop grieving for him. They'd had a wonderful life together, and then he died so quickly that she had no chance to say good-bye.

On the other hand, Lillian had some very good friends like

Josie who called her nearly every day. And she received many letters and cards, as well as invitations to dinner. Everybody's tried to keep me busy, she thought, I'm lucky to have such good friends.

"Yet I discovered our finances were in a terrible state," Lillian recalled. "Frank always paid the bills, and after his death I discovered we'd been living on savings ever since his company went bankrupt." Fortunately the house was paid for, but she would have to get a job if she wanted to keep it. Otherwise she couldn't afford the taxes and utilities nor even be able to buy food.

Lillian visited the vocational office at the college and found a helpful counselor who suggested she use her computer skills. She was able to get a great job working for a law firm where she would receive health benefits and a pension.

With her money problem solved, Lillian decided to begin writing Frank's biography. She wanted their children and grandchildren to know what a brave man he had been. "He served in two wars," she said, "and they should know."

Lillian had major stressors with the loss of her husband and her financial problems. Her bereavement was a stressor she couldn't change. The only control she had was in her response to it. In this context, her happy memories and her positive attitudes toward getting on with her life were helpful. Predictions about her job situation, taking control of her personal and work life, and using social supports were positive factors in reducing her stress level. Writing the story of Frank's life provided an outlet for reliving her memories and the sadness that their life together was over.

In summary, dealing with the stresses that come with living is an important task for maintaining and improving memory skills. Stress not only limits attention and concentration but also inflicts physical damage on the brain centers involved with memory.

Reduce Depression to Improve Memory

Probably everyone reading this book can remember the experience of feeling blue—this is part of the human condition. People deal with the blues in their own ways—a hike through the woods or by the seashore, lunch with a friend, a yummy dinner at a special restaurant, or off to bed with a book by a favorite author.

Depression, as contrasted with a simple case of the blues, too may lift with one of these time-honored approaches, but depression often takes longer to dissipate and may entail greater personal suffering.

Depression is the most common cause of memory problems as people grow older. This is an illness which, in part, may be the body's response to the multiple stresses of the later years.

A person who is depressed may process events so shallowly that they do not register. This state of mind prevents the attention and concentration required for normal memory functioning.

People have described depression as feeling numb. "Why bother?" they ask. "Nothing makes any difference." Symptoms of depression are:

- memory problems
- inability to experience positive feelings
- low energy
- a helpless-hopeless state of mind
- difficulty in concentrating and making even simple decisions
- lack of appetite or overeating
- sleep disorders, either difficulty in going to sleep or

sleeping more than usual
- preoccupation with death

Depressed people may stay at home with curtains drawn. When they are with others, they may sit silently so no one suspects anything is wrong. Others become overly vocal and complain a lot.

Depression destroys the quality of life. When people give up on living, their state of mind may become life-threatening. Fortunately, with appropriate treatment the condition is reversible. And when the depression lifts, memory skills return.

Marie Oliver was worried that her husband John might have Alzheimer's Disease. He had attended two memory training classes, but they didn't seem to help him.

She finally discussed her concern with their doctor. "John just seems out of it a lot of the time, she said. He doesn't remember the simplest things I tell him. He just sits in his old chair like a bump on a log."

She mentioned that she and John had seen a movie the previous day. When our son asked about it, John couldn't remember what the movie was or anything about it, she continued.

"He has trouble sleeping and wanders around the house at night. I'm afraid he'll fall down the stairs."

"It could be any one of a number of things," the doctor told her. He said he'd order tests to try to determine the problem.

Extensive testing showed that John's problem was depression. The doctor recommended medication and counseling.

John later told a friend that six months earlier his mind had been like a sieve. "Now my memory is as good as it ever was. The doc gave me some great medication and suggested Marie and I go out more and try to find things we enjoy doing together. I guess we were getting in a rut."

John felt as if he had a whole new lease on life.

Other steps you can take to help alleviate depression include:

- Exercise daily. Exercise releases chemicals in your body that help combat depression.
- Avoid alcohol. Alcohol works as a depressant.
- Check with your pharmacist to insure you are not taking a medication that contributes to depression. If you are, discuss this with your doctor.
- Practice a healthy regimen of diet and sleep.
- Spend time with other people. Perhaps join a support group.
- Get plenty of sunshine. Recent studies suggest that exposure to sunshine is a mood-elevator.

As John and many others have discovered, depression is reversible.

Exercises:
Take a Personal Stress and Depression Inventory

1. On a sheet of paper, list the things in your life that cause you to feel stressed. Number them according to the degree of stress with number 1 being the most stressful.
2. Put a check mark next to the stresses you feel you handle well.
3. Put an X next to the stresses which seem difficult to cope with.
4. Identify the control you have for each of the items you placed an X next to.
   What are you doing now?
   What else could you do?
   What do you need help with?
5. Do you have family or friends with whom you can share your experiences and feelings? If so, are you taking advantage of this resource? If not what can you do to develop such relationships?
6. List outlets you have for your personal energies that you might use to ease your stress:

   • Study?
   • Exercise?
   • Helping others?
   • Creating something?
   • Writing your life history?
   • Hobbies?
   • Other?

7. Do you have any or several of the symptoms of depression listed on pages 150–151? Do you ever feel that your life doesn't seem worth living? If so, have you discussed this with your doctor or a counselor?

8. Do you occasionally worry about a specific problem which might be resolved or alleviated simply by getting more information or advice? If so, what type?

- Business services?
- Legal services?
- Spiritual support?
- Counseling for an objective perspective?
- Other?

Your local Office on Aging has an information and referral service which may be helpful. (See Resources page 185.)

9. Do you plan to take any action as the result of information in this chapter? If so, what?

NINE

Understand and Cope with the Natural Aging Process

A UTUMN, WITH ITS RICHLY-COLORED landscapes delighting the eye, is nature's harvest season. The correlating period in our lives, our fifties or sixties, is the time for us to harvest the fruits of our life experiences, enjoy our maturity, and celebrate our successes.

This is the period when many of us first begin to feel anxious about memory lapses. Granted, men and women of all ages miss appointments, neglect to pay bills on time, have "tip of the tongue" experiences, and forget items like shopping lists. Yet from middle age on, people complain they forget things they didn't forget before.

Research indicates that there are some changes in memory functioning as you grow older. Yet these changes can be more than compensated for. In fact, your age alone does not predict how well you remember things. That, as we have seen, is closely related to your motivation, habits of attention, concentration, and the way you organize information, together with reasonably good health.

A significant factor in a healthy lifestyle is to adapt to and cope with whatever physical problems may occur. Being alert to changes in your ability to see and hear what is happening around you is an important part of this process.

Age-Related Sensory Changes

Sensory traces often provide the first step to forming and recalling a memory. However, age and life experiences tend to reduce the acuity of all of our senses. Changes in vision and hearing may cause indistinct or distorted sensory traces. Since it is these memory traces that determine how we perceive what we are experiencing, our memory of the related event is affected.

In driving, for example, misreading a street sign on a freeway or not having heard directions correctly can take you many miles out of your way.

PROBLEMS WITH VISION

The first sign of an age-related change for many people in middle life is the need to squint to read the telephone book. This is a good reminder of the necessity for an examination by an ophthalmologist, a medical doctor, who in addition to prescribing glasses can check for any eye disorders.

Cataracts are a leading source of vision problems as people grow older. A cataract is a gradual clouding of the normally clear lens of the eye causing blurred or double vision, increased sensitivity to light and glare, and halos around lights.

A major reason for this condition seems to be cumulative exposure to the ultraviolet rays of the sun and possibly to other radiation. Smoking, eye injury, and genetic defects are other possible causes.

You can obtain a degree of protection against cataracts by wearing sunglasses which block at least ninety-five percent of the ultraviolet B rays of the sun. Some research indicates that there is a tie between cataracts and nutrition and that antioxidants such as vitamins C, E, and A offer additional protection.

People often live with cataracts for a long time. When the cataracts become so opaque as to interfere with the activities of daily life, surgery is recommended. Today the procedure is relatively simple. It involves removing the lens and either replacing it with an implant or prescribing special glasses.

Glaucoma also is more common as people grow older. In this condition, there is increased fluid pressure within the eye which damages the retina, the lining of the inner eye that sends the image of what you're seeing to the brain. Diagnosis and treatment of glaucoma is essential to protect vision.

The reason for routine eye examinations is that the most common type of glaucoma usually has no symptoms in its early stages. The manifestation of the disease involves a gradual loss of peripheral vision and increasing blind spots. The rarer type is caused by a rapid buildup of fluid within the eye resulting in severe eye pain, nausea, and the perception of rainbow-colored halos around lights. This is an emergency requiring immediate medical attention.

Most specialists recommend a complete eye examination at least every two years after age fifty.

In contrast to the effects of glaucoma, macular degeneration involves the loss of central vision, necessary for reading and close work. It may progress very slowly so there is no sudden severe loss of vision. If you suffer such symptoms as difficulty in reading, blurring or blank spots in central vision, or the perception of bends in straight lines, you should discuss them with your doctor.

Early treatment for macular degeneration may be critical to preserving vision. Some research has shown that antioxidants may protect against macular degeneration as well as cataracts.

Diabetics are particularly at risk for eye damage to blood vessels in the retina. Because of the importance of early diagnosis and treatment, every diabetic should be examined by an ophthalmologist at intervals specified by a doctor.

PROBLEMS WITH HEARING

We garner much of our new information from what we hear. Communication with other people and our understanding of their world depends almost entirely on hearing. People with severe hearing deficits may not only be misinformed but also have incorrect memories of some events. Over time they may come to feel uncertain which memories are accurate. A reluctance to cause others inconvenience by asking them to repeat what they said may result in the further breakdown of communication and affect the quality of daily living.

> On the first day of a memory class, David Windsor said, "I'm here because my wife said I had to come. I lost my memory forty years ago."
>
> During the following six sessions, he participated in discussions and seemed to have no problem either with short term memory or remembering material from previous sessions.
>
> At the final session, David said, "There's something I'd like to share with the class. We've been learning about all the things that affect memory. Well, I've discovered I never did lose my memory forty years ago. What I did was decide that because of my hearing problem I would never again ask anyone to repeat something I hadn't heard the first time. So a lot of what people have been saying I didn't forget. I just never learned.
>
> "From now on I'm going to change all that. I'm not going to be afraid to ask my family and my friends to repeat things when I can't hear them."

Two weeks later his wife telephoned. "I want you to know that since David discovered that his problem was not his memory but a hearing problem, our entire family life has changed. He seems happier than he's been in years—so much more involved with family and his friends."

Severe hearing problems isolate people, who are likely to feel like outsiders and spend more and more time alone. Compensating for or correcting hearing loss to the greatest extent possible is an important way of keeping in touch with friends and learning what is going on in the world. Unfortunately, some hearing losses are not easily corrected and require perseverance to get the best possible help.

Some men and women have learned sign language to compensate for severe hearing deficits. People who refuse to be limited by their problem may form a group for lectures or school programs and hire an interpreter, who stands beside a speaker and repeats the lecture in sign language. This procedure has worked well in memory training classes held at a senior center with a club for the hearing impaired.

People with hearing losses often have difficulty making sense of what they are hearing when several conversations are occurring in the same room. John Williams developed a plan to deal with this problem and, as a result, to enjoy quality time with the people he loved.

John and Barbara Williams had five children and loved having them all together on the rare occasions when they could get away from their jobs and in-laws. John had a hearing loss caused by the firing of artillery. But he had developed a plan to avoid being distracted by the confusion which always occurred in family gatherings.

He would sit silently watching, as, all talking at once, they brought each other up to date on what had been going on since their last visit.

Then one by one he would take them off to his den to hear about what was going on in their lives, their new ideas, and what had changed for them since their last visit. In this way, he kept up to date and also was able to spend quality time with each child. Time he could remember and savor after they had all gone.

John had a reputation as the family chronicler. As one of the grandchildren said, "Who needs a calendar when grandad's around?" John became deeply involved in whatever interested him and remembered the smallest details about the children.

Barbara used him as her authority on birthdays and the grandchildren's activities. She could always count on John to know the names of all the children's friends. He was a gold mine at Christmas because he always knew the best gift for each member of the family.

Barbara sometimes wondered why he had such a good memory and decided it was because of the concentration he had learned to give to everything in order to compensate for his hearing problem.

John is a good example of someone with a stressful problem taking charge of his life and developing a super memory to compensate for his disability.

Although problems with the other senses like smell and touch may affect the quality of your life, they seldom materially affect the memory process. If you cannot smell the oyster stew at the Grand Central Oyster Bar, thereby missing some of the pleasure, you can still appreciate and remember other aspects of lunching there.

However, some other accompaniments of aging have a more direct impact on memory.

Memory Changes with Aging

Normal aging affects memory because of three factors:

- slowing of the central nervous system
- increasing distractibility
- shallow processing of information, in contrast to in-depth thought

The good news is that the many things detailed in this book to help you maintain and improve your memory can more than compensate for these changes.

SLOWING OF THE CENTRAL NERVOUS SYSTEM

If you know people in their late eighties and older, you have probably noted the slow pace of their speech, movement, and thinking. This slowing is the end result of many years of an exceedingly gradual reduction in the rate of nerve functioning. This process involves every part of the nervous system including sensory and motor nerves, as well as the thought process itself.

Such slowing may come into play in a situation where you are being introduced to strangers. If your hostess speaks rapidly, you and the others may not have enough time to make connections between names and faces. You can deal with this problem by setting your own pace and focusing on one person at a time. Recognizing that slowing is a fact of life for everyone and then accepting it should enable you to feel comfortable with it. As a result, you will remember more than if some of your consciousness is involved with feeling inadequate. Later on, if you ask people for their names, your openness about your inability to register names quickly may elicit, "I know what you mean. I couldn't catch everyone's name either."

This slowing of the central nervous system can be a safety issue for people driving automobiles or operating machinery. The 55 Alive mature driver training, sponsored by the American Association of Retired Persons, was developed to address problems which accompany normal aging. In the program, people over fifty-five are challenged to remember and use safe driving practices.

Taking longer to see a red light or stop sign and longer to respond to it require changes in driving habits if people are to avoid accidents. The program emphasizes the importance of remembering to think ahead. The value of the program is reflected both in the responses of participants and in the fact that insurance companies give discounts on premiums to people who take the class every three years.

INCREASING DISTRACTIBILITY

In the process of daily living, we all get distracted from time to time. This is true for the 27-year-old as well as the 77-year-old. However, distractibility seems to be more of a problem as people grow older. Driving an automobile is hazardous for people who use their travel time for bird-watching or an absorbing discussion of some issue with their passenger. These and similar things may be so distracting that there is little attention available for driving safely.

Conversation seems to be more distracting than nonverbal sounds. Music or traffic noises do not seem to be as bothersome, unless you deliberately turn your attention to a particular sound or tune, or the sound is so loud it drowns out what you need to hear.

Distraction is common when several discussions are going on at once. This is often a problem at large gatherings with people milling about. Under these circumstances, it's easy to become distracted to the point of forgetfulness.

A different problem occurs when you distract yourself by letting your attention wander.

Joan Sanders wants to check her calendar to see what day is free next week to take her granddaughter Suzie to the zoo. The calendar is always on top of the desk in her study at the other end of the house.

She glances at the ceiling as she walks out the kitchen door and thinks, I must speak to Margaret next week about brushing down the cobwebs. As a matter of fact, the kitchen really needs painting. Well maybe next fall... I wonder if I could find a good painter who's less expensive than Black & White. I must ask Sally who she got to do her house.

Then, as she passes the window: Why that's Barbara going down the street. I haven't seen her in ages. I'll bet her new grandchild is about due. Her yard always looks so colorful. I think I'll go over to the nursery and pick up a few plants to put in that bed by the front door. This is the day Alan comes to dinner. He loves to garden, and I'm sure he'll put them in for me.

By this time, she has entirely forgotten what she wanted from the study.

Joan's attention was distracted as she walked through the house rather than being focused on her goal. She distracted herself. She could have stayed focused. Her situation suggests a model for taking charge of your attention with:

- A thought: "Suzie has school until one o'clock every day," or "Having my calendar on the desk is the most convenient place for it."
- A feeling: "I love watching Suzie at the zoo," or "I feel good about keeping my calendar on the desk. I always know where it is."
- An action: Joan could say the word "calendar" once or twice on the way to her study.

Anytime you're speaking, you may be distracted by a passing thought only slightly related to the subject under discussion. You may even go off on a tangent until someone draws you back to the appropriate topic. This occurs because of a wealth of possible connections in everyone's memory bank. You can train yourself to become aware of distracting thoughts as they appear and to return promptly to your current subject by recognizing the problem exists and by focusing on what you are saying.

We also distract ourselves with personal concerns unrelated to what is happening. In a conversation with several people, you might suddenly think, Tonight would be a good night for steak, and I'd better leave here early if I'm to catch the butcher. Or you may be repeating the thought you had on leaving home, I really should have paid my bills last night.

Once again, becoming aware of how and under what circumstances you are distracted and how you distract yourself are important insights. You can then decide either to go with the distraction or to stay focused on what you were doing.

Putting this decision into practice requires a commitment of time and patience in order to create a new style of responding to the events of everyday living. However, avoiding distractions, both external and internal, can contribute greatly to preventing the stress of memory lapses. It also can permit in-depth processing of new ideas.

SHALLOW VERSUS IN-DEPTH THINKING

Shallow processing of information is like reading a newspaper by simply scanning the headlines without reading the articles. Without an in-depth look at the news, the information in the headlines is often forgotten. An in-depth treatment would entail reading the story and thinking about the causes and implications of the events covered and the meanings behind these events for you and your world.

In the same way, sensory impressions and passing thoughts drift away when no meaningful connections are made with other data in your memory bank. This pattern fails to create the variety of memory traces which make information memorable. A result is such comments as, "I can't remember what you said you were going to be doing today," or, "Somebody called and left you a message. I've forgotten who it was."

This kind of memory problem seems to be more common as we age. Boredom or disinterest are logical and valid reasons for such shallow processing of new information, but these excuses do nothing to provide the mental exercise needed to keep your memory skills honed.

Lack of in-depth thinking has a direct impact on forgetting anything—names, conversations, appointments, and obligations or details of daily living. When you don't tie it to other data or examine such factors as meaning, cause and effect, comparison and contrast, memory lapses often occur.

When you want to remember something, the solution is to focus and think in-depth about that new information, to give it your full attention, and to make one or more connections. This collection and integration of information will supply the multiple traces which create memories. If you want to remember the article, read more than the headline.

A lifestyle based on enthusiasm for learning stimulates in-depth thinking and supports a good memory. And learning and memory, like physical skills, become stronger with exercise.

- If you are fascinated by ancient history, you will be quick at comparing trends and noting the implications of what is taking place today in the Middle East.
- If you find arts and crafts fascinating, you may spend hours studying designs and fabrics from various cultures in Africa, comparing them with others you've seen and wondering how you can use them yourself.

Whatever is meaningful you will think about often and remember. This approach enables older adults to learn and remember as well as younger people.

Exercises:
Confront Age-related Memory Issues

1. Have you ever had memory problems which were, in fact, visual problems or hearing problems?
2. Are there additional actions you can take which will safeguard your vision?
3. Are there new actions you can take which will benefit your hearing?
4. Do you feel comfortable with the pacing of your life? If not, how might you go about making changes?
5. Do you often feel distracted in groups of people? If so, can you think of ways to compensate for this?
6. In what situations do you distract yourself? What steps would lead to less self-distraction?
7. How might you take charge of external distractions you experience?
8. Has shallow processing of news reports left you without information you wished you had?
9. What subjects of in-depth study would be meaningful for you?

TEN

Become
Your Own Mentor

I N *THE WAY OF MAN*, MARTIN BUBER tells the story of Rabbi Zusya on his death bed. Zusya is lamenting his life because he says he knows that when he gets to heaven, God will not ask why he was not like Moses. Rather God will say, "Why were you not like Zusya?"

Like Zusya, you may wish you were more like the person you have the potential for being. This memory program of *"ten simple things you can do…"* is designed to help you reach that potential.

Your best ally in this is a mentor, a wise and trustworthy advisor and guide who supports your desire to improve your memory. *You* can be this mentor.

QUALITIES AND GIFTS OF A MENTOR
Everyone can develop an inner mentor, a mentor that will assist you to:

- think and act logically and realistically
- provide caring self-support
- free up your natural energies for memory duty
- set reasonable limits in working toward your goals

These are all natural capabilities which have already been active to some degree as you read this book and thought about implementing your own memory program. You can decide to use them more often and in specific situations where you want to enhance your memory.

A mentor will provide firm support and encouraging messages to help you develop these four qualities which, in turn, will help you to build a better memory. Such a mentor will supply you with three assets: permission, protection, and potency.

- permission to grow toward your full potential
- protection against whatever would interfere with this process
- a sense of potency from the experience of working toward and reaching your personal goals

Permission is an essential gift from a wise mentor. Your inner mentor will give you permission to cultivate positive attitudes toward building a better memory. These will be based on self-acceptance as a person-in-process who is continuing to grow through working toward meaningful goals.

Positive attitudes and self-acceptance will enable you to make the kinds of changes needed to enhance your memory.

PERMISSION
Your mentor-self can give you permission to think in realistic ways and to answer for yourself such questions as:

- What are my priorities for building a better memory?
- Are my goals reasonable? If not, how do I need to change them?
- Is my plan for reaching them logical and practical?
- Do I need to use more or less self-discipline?

- Why do I seem never to have enough time? Or energy?
- Do I need more time for me? Just to be me?
- What do I need to do in order to have more positive experiences in my life?

Don Welsh and a number of his friends formed a group to give moral support to each other as they launched their individual memory programs. At one of the first gatherings they discussed the permissions they planned to give themselves to reduce memory lapses. Some of their remarks were:

"I'm giving myself permission not to feel old or guilty if I forget something. I've been getting to be a real worrywart about my memory. But everybody forgets sometimes—even my grandchildren."

"I'm going to give myself permission to spend a little part of every day just on myself."

"My problem is I'm too lazy to organize my desk. I'm always forgetting where I put things. Last month I paid my club dues twice and forgot all about the garbage bill. I need to give myself permission to get organized. Wow...that feels great just thinking about it!"

"I need to take my time. I'm always in a rush, so, of course, I forget things. I just have too many irons in the fire. I'm giving myself permission to resign two of my volunteer jobs when the terms run out this fall. Then I'll be able to stop feeling so pressured that I get distracted."

"If I'm feeling blue, I get really low on energy. I'm going to give myself permission, when I'm feeling that way, to go for a walk or read something interesting so I can move out of that negative space."

"I'm interested in this idea of monologue masquerading as dialogue. I admit when someone is talking to me, I'm often thinking about what I'll say next. I've been giving myself permission to concentrate on what other people are saying, even if it means I'll have to pause for a moment before answering."

PROTECTION

Protection is the second quality which your inner mentor can provide. It may mean defending you against attitudes and lifestyle habits which interfere with honing your memory skills.

An example is the way some of us deal with our health problems. The recognition that physical, mental, and emotional health are critical factors in building a better memory should give good health high priority in a memory program. Unfortunately, many of us procrastinate or ignore this.

Self-mentoring will ensure you get the best medical advice. In many cases, this means obtaining a second opinion—often well worth the time and money it may require.

Your mentor might make you aware of ways you sabotage your health maintenance program. This may include alerting you to poor diet habits, to shortfalls in your physical and mental exercise, or to a loosening of your weight control program. Your inner mentor will help you minimize your exposure to toxins.

Procrastination can sink the best intentions. A wise mentor-self will help you recognize and deal with this when it interferes with issues important to you and your memory program.

Protecting you against damage from severe or chronic stress may be an important task for your mentor. Developing some sense of how you can control your responses to the stresses of your life may start with the implementation of stress reduction techniques. Your mentor may be creative in analyzing the degree of control you can exert, the kind of support you need, and outlets for your negative feelings.

In periods of acute stress, your mentor might suggest you seek professional advice to deal with worry, anxiety, depression, or grief. In less severe situations, your mentor may suggest a long, hot bath or a few minutes sitting quietly listening to your favorite music. Your mentor may suggest setting aside a block of time each day to do just what you want to do.

As you work toward your memory goals, your mentor may alert you to feelings which consistently trip you up. These feelings may be in response to overly self-critical or self-indulgent attitudes that can sabotage your memory project.

Do you repeatedly experience a negative feeling in certain situations? If so, your mentor might point out that this feeling is now invalid and perhaps always has been.

For instance, some people tell themselves:

- "I'll never be able to do it."
- "Nothing ever goes right for me."
- "I'm too stupid to learn that."
- "I'm old. What should I expect?"

A realistic view of these and similar pessimistic and self-defeating messages often show that they are delusions. Good protection against such negative attitudes is to recall instances when you have been successful—even very successful—in reaching your goals.

Nurturing optimism within yourself and spending time with others who have similar positive attitudes will reinforce your position.

In addition to dealing with internal issues, your mentor has a role in protecting you from external factors creating unwelcome distractions. These can range from clutter in your surroundings to excessive demands on your energies. Your mentor can encourage you to organize your environment and reduce the energy spent in activities which interfere with attention to your priorities.

POTENCY

Potency is the third gift from a mentor who is supportive and sets reasonable limits. Taking charge of your life in significant ways increases your sense of personal potency.

Many opportunities exist for the mentor part of your personality to increase your potency as you:

- commit yourself to setting goals
- design plans to implement them
- adapt your plans as experience suggests
- persist in working with them until your goals are reached

Your mentor might help you increase your sense of potency through budgeting time so that you have enough quality time for your priorities. As a result, you can avoid the feelings of inadequacy or the pitfalls that accompany trying to deal with too many things at once.

In providing permission, protection, and potency, your personal mentor can contribute greatly to the success of your program for improving your memory. In the process, you will gain from being increasingly familiar with your own memory at work and with your unique style of being and doing.

CONTRACTS

Your mentor can help to increase your personal potency by suggesting contracts for you to make with yourself. A contract formalizes your decision to adopt a specific habit, a way of thinking, or a course of action. Contracts are a tool for taking control.

Contracts may be designed around health issues, such as exercise or diet. Or they may deal with internal or external distractions. A contract may be directed at creating a time management program to leave more time for recreation. Or it might involve limiting commitments or finding new interests. Inherent in any contract is a commitment to vanquish personal actions or nonactions that could sabotage your plan.

An effective contract is reasonable and practical and avoids either the overly simple or the grandiose. The results of a contract should be measurable.

For instance, a contract that states, "I will have a perfect memory," is not reasonable because remembering every thought entering your mind is neither possible nor advisable.

"I will improve my memory for taking my medicine," is not measurable. A contract that is measurable would be: "Before dinner tonight I will develop a plan for remembering to take my medicine and will review and write it down so I won't forget it."

Some other reasonable and measurable contracts are:

"I will place all meetings and appointments on the calendar and check it every morning."

"When I go to the party on Saturday, I will leave my worries about ___ at home."

"I will see that my bills are paid on time by writing checks on the first and fifteenth of the month. Notations on my calendar for the year, made by January 1, will remind me."

"When I am talking with a friend, I will focus on what he is saying instead of thinking about what I am going to say next. If my mind wanders, I will refocus my attention."

The model for designing an effective contract is:

1. What do I want?
2. What will have to change to get it?
3. What am I willing to do?
4. How might I sabotage the contract?
5. How can I prevent that?
6. How will I know when the contract is completed?

Going back over the exercises at the end of each chapter may suggest to you some specific ways in which you can design your contracts. Selection of an objective you can achieve fairly soon will encourage you to continue on to tasks which present greater challenges.

Fulfilling a contract is cause for celebration and provides the encouragement for moving on to more challenging contracts.

Identifying goals and working toward them in this realistic fashion will enhance both your quality of life and the effectiveness of your memory.

Exercises:
Create Your First Self-Contract

Answer the following to create a contract with yourself:
1. What problem do I have that is affecting memory?
2. What action could I take so this is no longer a problem?
3. The contract: What am I willing to do?
4. How might I sabotage this contract?
5. How can I prevent such sabotage?
6. How will I know when this contract is completed?

Summary

As you progress with your memory project, you may want to review parts or the whole of this memory program. The following summary of its ten elements is a useful tool for this purpose:

1. Understand how your memory works.
2. Equip your memory tool chest.
3. Find the motivation and commit yourself.
4. Enjoy life and continue to grow.
5. Increase your power to focus.
6. Organize your learning and your life.
7. Take care of your health.
8. Deal with stress and depression.
9. Understand and cope with the natural aging process.
10. Become your own mentor.

UNDERSTAND HOW YOUR MEMORY WORKS

Understanding how memory works will give you insight into ways of taking control in order to increase your memory power. A summary of the major factors involved in memory functioning:

- Memory is the process of registering, consolidating, storing, and recalling information and also is the result of that process.
- Memory is an electrochemical process of the brain and nervous system in which specialized brain centers receive, consolidate, store, and respond to new information.
- The more memory traces you amass from sensory experiences, thoughts, feelings, and actions, the more ways you have to recall a particular piece of information.
- A stimulating environment makes a major contribution to improving your memory.
- People learn incidentally in the process of living and intentionally through deliberate study.
- New information becomes a memory by moving from sensory memory to short-term memory. There working memory creates the connections to consolidate it into long-term memory.
- Memory contains two kinds of material: knowledge—both general and personal—and procedures. Procedures do not require conscious attention in order to function.

Equip Your Memory Tool Chest

Natural abilities which you can use to maintain and improve your memory are:

- sensory awareness
- mental images
- words and messages

- making associations and connections
- grouping
- repetition
- rehearsal and review
- spacing
- using memory aids as reminders

Sensory awareness involves collecting information from your senses to amass the memory traces which help you remember people, places, or events.

Mental imaging is to visualize in your mind an image of something or someone you want to remember.

Words can be used to help you remember in a number of ways. Talking to yourself creates verbal memory traces. Acronyms, rhymes, or jingles may help jog your memory.

Making new connections is the process which relates new information to what you already know thereby making the new information easier to recall.

Sorting and grouping are ways of categorizing data to provide memory traces to aid in recall. Relationships among major groups and among the items in each subgroup create the connections which make all items memorable.

Repetition helps you to hold information in your short term memory as your working memory organizes and integrates it into long term memory.

Rehearsal and review, both reinforced by repetition, help you to remember tasks or events that will take place in the future and to recall information or events from the past.

Spacing is the practice of leaving intervals between learning sessions in order to reinforce memory traces.

Memory aids are concrete reminders—notes, calendars, pill safes—which help you remember. Other people may also be effective memory aids if they have ways of remembering to remind you.

FIND THE MOTIVATION AND COMMIT YOURSELF

Improving your memory relies on motivation. When people are motivated, they pay attention and concentrate in order to consolidate what they are experiencing into lasting memories. When people are motivated, they often set goals.

The Muriel and John James model demonstrates that we are motivated by seven urges which push us toward goals. These urges are: the urge to live, with goals of survival, comfort, and to find meaning in living; the urge to be free with a goal of self-determination; the urge to enjoy with a goal of happiness; the urge to understand with a goal of knowledge; the urge to create with a goal of originality; the urge to connect with a goal of love; and the urge to transcend with a goal of unity.

Your goals for your memory project are determined by your goals for your life. In looking at the natural urges of all of us, you may choose to set goals related to your health or your lifestyle habits or you may decide to find greater meaning in the events and circumstances of your personal experiences. Often a desire for self-determination or a desire to be free of the discomfort of memory lapses works as the driving motivation for goal-setting.

Making the decision to work toward a goal frees up energy and allows you to become action-oriented. Yet like water in a river, energy necessary to reach goals may be limited by dams, drains, or constrictions. These limiters, such as illness, excess responsibilities, and worry, need to be identified and alleviated or eliminated.

Working toward your goals may require a variety of personal

resources including hope, courage, curiosity, imagination, enthusiasm, caring and concern, and an openness to new or different ideas.

In the end, motivation is the force behind the decisions, commitments, self-discipline, and patience required to reach your goals.

ENJOY LIFE AND CONTINUE GROWING

Your natural urges to enjoy, to understand, to create, to connect with others, and to transcend also may come into play as motivators in the execution of your memory project.

It is important to decide to enjoy living. But to do that you must deal with any pain or grief you are experiencing and move on.

Most of us have a natural curiosity about the world we live in and the people who populate it. This urge to understand can lead us to search for new information and to want to remember this information. Honing our skills in retaining what we read and hear and working to build on new information as we obtain it are important parts of a sound memory project. This natural learning goes on throughout our life.

Creativeness may be expressed in the arts, in our jobs, or even in how we make the bed in the morning. Memory is necessary in all creative projects, and being creative improves our memory capabilities automatically.

Connecting with others creates meaningful memories. But failure to pay attention and other factors often interfere with our relationships. As time progresses, old relationships sometimes need to be replaced with new ones. This often comes with challenges relating to shyness, to difficulty in getting around, and to being close-minded. Relationships add to the wealth of our lives and play an important part in our memory program.

The desire to transcend, to grow more whole with the years, and to use more of our potential is within us all. This urge is easier to satisfy if we are open to all the alternatives and possibilities our world has to offer.

INCREASE YOUR POWER TO FOCUS

Attention is essential for memory. Focusing your attention allows you to keep items in your mind as long as you choose. You are surrounded by external stimuli calling for your attention. They may be in conflict with internal sensations, thoughts, and feelings which also demand attention. Both external and internal distractions may interfere with memory.

To concentrate is to sustain attention while ignoring distractions and interferences. Strategies to deal with distractions and interferences are to increase your use of memory aids, develop strong habits of attention and concentration, focus on one thing at a time and to set your own pace. In this way, you can accumulate a great deal of information and relate it to what you already know. The new material then becomes a part of your long term memory.

ORGANIZE YOUR LEARNING AND YOUR LIFE

Your memory is already organized. Memory traces are stored in an organized fashion, and you recall incidents, people, and knowledge in organized units. Therefore, you more easily learn information that you have consciously organized.

To organize material is to think about it, to relate it to what you already know, and to take any necessary action. Further organize your learning by breaking complex learning tasks into manageable units.

Besides organizing your learning, organizing your time and your surroundings will improve your memory because there will be fewer items forgotten or mislaid, fewer appointments missed, and less clutter and other distractions in your daily life.

TAKE CARE OF YOUR HEALTH

Beginning at about age 30, there are slight cumulative changes in all body systems, including the brain and nervous system. In addition, any illness or disease can affect memory. Making a commitment to a health maintenance plan is essential for good memory functioning. This plan includes a balanced diet, exercise, minimizing contact with toxic substances, and having regular medical checkups.

Keeping mentally active—finding new ways of learning and new fields to explore—is as healthy for your brain and nervous system as physical exercise is for your body. Most learning does not take place in a classroom. Having one or more absorbing interests in which you are continuously acquiring new information can provide the challenges and activities on which to build and maintain a good memory.

DEAL WITH STRESS AND DEPRESSION

Moods and feelings affect memory. They will reinforce a related memory but can interfere with remembering other events. Strong feelings often distract your attention from what is currently going on around you.

When feelings such as fear, worry, or anger drain personal energy, finding ways to cope with the resulting stress, large or small, is essential to maintaining a good memory. Some of these ways are:

- possessing a sense of control
- progressive relaxation, meditation or prayer
- exercise
- gaining insight into the predictable outcome of that which is generating the stress
- social supports
- outlets for the emotional energy which accompanies stress

Your inner mentor who relies on reality-testing for making recommendations may be helpful in all of these tasks.

Understand and Cope with the Aging Process

Your age alone does not predict how well you remember. Memory is closely related to motivation levels, to habits of attention, to how organized you are and to your health.

However, dealing with any age-related sensory changes you encounter is essential. Good eyesight and hearing are both important to how well you remember. Any significant decline in either should be treated or compensated for.

Slowing of the central nervous system, increasing distractibility, and more shallow processing of information are all natural occurrences as we age. Each of these may be counterbalanced with recognition that they are a fact of life, with pacing ourselves, with concentration, and with in-depth thought and review and other strategies.

Become Your Own Mentor

Your inner mentor acts to provide support and guidance by supplying three assets: permission, protection, and potency. As a result, you can make the kinds of changes in attitudes and lifestyle which create a better memory.

Empowering this inner mentor will contribute greatly to your success in determining which memory tools and habits will be most effective for you and which memory aids will save time and prevent memory lapses.

Your mentor then will be supportive as you make the kinds of changes in your attitudes and lifestyle that will improve your memory. The contract is a useful tool for this purpose.

Resources

There are many organizations that supply information and assistance. Here is a partial listing. Call or write and ask to be put on the mailing list of any that interest you. Search the Internet, check your Yellow Pages or ask your health care professional or reference librarian for others.

American Association of
Retired Persons
601 E Street, N.W.
Washington, D.C. 20049
Pubications and conferences

Amerian Society on Aging
833 Market Street
San Francisco, CA 94103-1824
Publications and conferences

Elderhostel
75 Federal Street
Boston, MA 02100
Personal enrichment, education
and service programs

Older Women's League
666 11th Street, N.W.
Washington, D.C, 2001
Publications and conferences

The National Council on the
Aging
409 Third Street, S.W.
Washington, D.C. 20024
Publications and conferences

The National Council on Aging
Address Locator 1908A1
Ottawa, Ontario KIA 1B4
Canada
Publications and conferences

The National Self-Help
Clearinghouse
33 W. 42nd St.
New York, NY 10036
Locates local support groups

The Service Corps of Retired
Executives
Small Business Administration
409 3rd Street, S. W.
Washington, D.C. 20024

STATE DEPARTMENTS OF AGING

Alabama Commission on Aging
RSA Plaza, Suite 470
770 Washington Avenue
Montgomery, AL 36130
(334) 242-5743
FAX: (334) 242 5594

Alaska Commission on Aging
Division of Senior Services
Department of Administration
Juneau, AK 99811-0209
(907) 465-3250
FAX: (907) 465-4716

Aging and Adult Administration
Department of Economic Security
1789 West Jefferson Street -
#950A
Phoenix, AZ 85007
(602) 542-4446
FAX: (602) 542-6575

Division Aging and Adult Services
Arkansas Dept of Human Services
P.O. Box 1437, Slot 1412
7th and Main Streets
Little Rock, AR 72201
(501) 682-2441
FAX: (501) 682-8155

California Department of Aging
1600 K Street
Sacramento, CA 95814
(916) 322-5290
FAX: (916) 324-1903

Aging and Adult Services
Department of Social Services
110 16th Street, Suite 200
Denver, CO 80202-5202
(303) 620-4147
FAX: (303) 620-4189

Division of Elderly Services
25 Sigourney Street, 10th Floor
Hartford, CT 06106-5033
(860) 424-5277
FAX: (860) 424-4966

Delaware Division of Services for
Aging and Adults with Physical
Disabilities
Department of Health and
Social Services
1901 North DuPont Highway
New Castle, DE 19720
(302) 577-4791
FAX: (302) 577-4793

District of Columbia Office on Aging
One Judiciary Square - 9th Floor
441 Fourth Street, N.W.
Washington, DC 20001
(202) 724-5622
FAX: (202) 724-4979

Department of Elder Affairs
Building B - Suite 152
4040 Esplanade Way
Tallahassee, FL 32399-7000
(904) 414-2000
FAX: (904) 414-2002

Division of Aging Services
Department of Human Resources
2 Peachtree Street N.E.
18th Floor
Atlanta, GA 30303
(404) 657-5258
FAX: (404) 657-5285

Division of Senior Citizens
Department of Public Health &
Social Services
P.O. Box 2816
Agana, Guam 96932
671-475-0263
FAX: 671-477-2930

Hawaii Executive Office on Aging
250 South Hotel Street, Suite 107
Honolulu, HI 96813
(808) 586-0100
FAX (808) 586-0185

Idaho Commission on Aging
3380 Americana Terrace Suite 120
Boise, ID 83706
(208) 334-3833
FAX: (208) 334-3033

Illinois Department on Aging
421 East Capitol Avenue, Suite 100
Springfield, IL 62701-1789
(217) 785-2870
Chicago Office: (312) 814-2630
FAX: (217) 785-4477

Bureau of Aging and In-Home Services
Division of Disability, Aging and Rehabilitative Services
Family and Social Services Admin.
402 W. Washington Street, #W454
P.O. Box 7083
Indianapolis, IN 46207-7083
(317) 232-7020
FAX: (317) 232-7867

Iowa Department of Elder
Affairs
Clemens Building, 3rd Floor
200 Tenth Street
Des Moines, IA 50309-3609
(515) 281-5187
FAX: (515) 281-4036

Department on Aging
New England Building
503 S. Kansas Ave.
Topeka, KS 66603-3404
(785)-296-4986
FAX: (785)-296-0256

Kentucky Division of Aging
Services
Cabinet for Human Resources
275 East Main Street, 6 West
Frankfort, KY 40621
(502) 564-6930
FAX: (502) 564-4595

Governor's Office of Elderly
Affairs
P.O. Box 80374
412 N 4th Street, 3rd Floor
Baton Rouge, LA 70802
(504) 342-7100
FAX: (504) 342-7133

Bureau of Elder and Adult
Services
Department of Human Services
35 Anthony Avenue
State House - Station #11
Augusta, ME 04333
(207) 624-5335
FAX: (207) 624-5361

Maryland Office on Aging
State Office Building, Room
1007
301 West Preston Street
Baltimore, MD 21201-2374
(410) 767-1100
FAX: (410) 333-7943

Massachusetts Executive Office
of Elder Affairs
One Ashburton Place, 5th Floor
Boston, MA 02108
(617) 727-7750
FAX: (617) 727-9368

Office of Services to the Aging
P.O. Box 30026
Lansing, MI 48909-8176
(517) 373-8230
FAX: (517) 373-4092

Minnesota Board on Aging
444 Lafayette Road
St. Paul, MN 55155-3843
(612) 296-2770
FAX: (612) 297-7855

Division of Aging and Adult
Services
750 State Street
Jackson, MS 39202
(601) 359-4925
FAX: (601) 359-4370

Division on Aging
Department of Social Services
P.O. Box 1337
615 Howerton Court
Jefferson City, MO 65102-1337
(573) 751-3082
FAX: (573) 751-8493

Senior and Long Term Care
Division
Department of Public Health &
Human Services
P.O. Box 4210
111 Sanders, Room 211
Helena, MT 59604
(406) 444-7788
FAX: (406) 444-7743

Department of Health and Human
Services/Division on Aging
P.O. Box 95044
301 Centennial Mall South
Lincoln, NE 68509-5044
(402) 471-2307
FAX: (402) 471-4619

Nevada Division for Aging Services
Department of Human Resources
State Mail Room Complex
340 North 11th Street Suite 203
Las Vegas, NV 89101
(702) 486-3545
FAX: (702) 486-3572

Division of Elderly and Adult Services
State Office Park South
115 Pleasant Street, Annex Bldg. #1
Concord, NH 03301-3843
(603) 271-4680
FAX: (603) 271-4643

Department of Health and Senior
Services/Division of Senior Affairs
P.O Box 807
Trenton, New Jersey 08625-0807
(609) 588-3141
1-800-792-8820
FAX: (609) 588-3601

State Agency on Aging
La Villa Rivera Building, 4th
Floor
224 East Palace Avenue
Santa Fe, NM 87501
(505) 827-7640
FAX: (505) 827-7649

New York State Office for The
Aging
2 Empire State Plaza
Albany, NY 12223-1251
1-800-342-9871
(518) 474-5731
FAX: (518) 474-0608

Division of Aging
CB 29531
693 Palmer Drive
Raleigh, NC 27626-0531
(919) 733-3983
FAX: (919) 733-0443

Department of Human Services
Aging Services Division
600 South 2n Street, Suite 1C
Bismarck, ND 58504
(701) 328-8910
FAX: (701) 328-8989

CNMI Office on Aging
P.O. Box 2178
Commonwealth of the Northern
Mariana Islands
Saipan, MP 96950
(670) 233-1320/1321
FAX: (670) 233-1327/0369

Ohio Department of Aging
50 West Broad Street - 9th Floor
Columbus, OH 43215-5928
(614) 466-5500
FAX: (614) 466-5741

Services for the Aging
Department of Human Services
P.O. Box 25352
312 N.E. 28th Street
Oklahoma City, OK 73125
(405) 521-2281 or 521-2327
FAX: (405) 521-2086

Senior and Disabled Services
Division
500 Summer Street, N.E., 2nd
Floor
Salem, OR 97310-1015
(503) 945-5811
FAX: (503) 373-7823

State Agency on Aging
Republic of Palau
Koror, PW 96940
9-10-288-011-680-488-2736
FAX: 9-10-288-011-680-488-
1662

Pennsylvania Department of
Aging
Commonwealth of Pennsylvania
555 Walnut Street, 5th floor
Harrisburg, PA 17101-1919
(717) 783-1550
FAX: (717) 772-3382

Commonwealth of Puerto Rico
Governor's Office of Elderly
Affairs
Call Box 50063
Old San Juan Station, PR 00902
(787) 721-5710
FAX: (787) 721-6510

Department of Elderly Affairs
160 Pine Street
Providence, RI 02903-3708
(401) 277-2858
FAX: (401) 277-2130

Territorial Administration on
Aging/Government of
American Samoa
Pago Pago, American Samoa 96799
011-684-633-2207
FAX: 011-684-633-2533

Office on Aging
South Carolina Department of
Health and Human Services
P.O. Box 8206
Columbia, SC 29201-8206
(803) 253-6177
FAX: (803) 253-4173

Office of Adult Services and
Aging
Richard F. Kneip Building
700 Governors Drive
Pierre, SD 57501-2291
(605) 773-3656
FAX: (605) 773-6834

Commission on Aging
Andrew Jackson Building. 9th floor,
500 Deaderick Street,
Nashville, Tennessee 37243
(615) 741-2056
FAX: (615) 741-3309

Texas Department on Aging
4900 North Lamar, 4th Floor
Austin, TX 78751
(512) 424-6840
FAX: (512) 424-6890

Division of Aging & Adult
Services
Box 45500
120 North 200 West
Salt Lake City, UT 84145-0500
(801) 538-3910
FAX: (801) 538-4395

Vermont Department of Aging
and Disabilities
Waterbury Complex
103 South Main Street
Waterbury, VT 05676
(802) 241-2400
FAX: (802) 241-2325

Virginia Department for the
Aging
1600 Forest Avenue, Suite 102
Richmond, VA 23219-2327
(804) 662-9333
FAX: (804) 662-9354

Senior Citizen Affairs
Virgin Islands Department of
Human Services
Knud Hansen Complex,
Building A
1303 Hospital Ground
Charlotte Amalie, VI 00802
(809) 774-0930
FAX: (809) 774-3466

Aging and Adult Services
Administration
Department of Social & Health
Services
P.O. Box 45050
Olympia, WA 98504-5050
(360) 586-8753
FAX: (360) 902-7848

West Virginia Bureau
of Senior Services
Holly Grove - Building 10
1900 Kanawha Boulevard East
Charleston, WV 25305-0160
(304) 558-3317
FAX: (304) 558-0004

Bureau of Aging and Long Term
Care Resources
Department of Health and
Family Services
P.O. Box 7851
Madison, WI 53707
(608) 266-2536
FAX: (608) 267-3203

Wayne Milton, Program Coordinator
Office on Aging
Department of Health
117 Hathaway Building, Room 139
Cheyenne, WY 82002-0480
(307) 777-7986
FAX: (307) 777-5340

Bibliography

Ackerman, Diane. *A Natural History of the Senses*. Vintage Books, New York, 1990.

Armstrong, Thomas. *7 Kinds of Smart*. Plume, Penguin, New York, 1993.

Baddeley, Alan. *Your Memory: A User's Guide*. Avery Publishing Group, Garden City Park, N.Y., 1993.

Barnard, Neal. *Eat Right, Live Longer*. Crown, New York, 1995.

Beers, Mark H. and Stephen K. Urice. *Aging in Good Health: A Complete Essential Medical Guide for Older Men and Women and Their Families*. Pocket Books, New York, 1992.

Benson, Herbert, M.D. *The Relaxation Response*. Avon, New York, 1975.

Buber, Martin. *I and Thou*. Charles Scribner's Sons, New York, 1958.

———. *The Way of Man*. The Citadel Press, New York, 1970.

Carper, Jean. *Stop Aging Now!* Harper Perennial, New York, 1995.

Colgrove, Melba, Harold H. Bloomfield and Peter McWilliams. *How To Survive the Loss of a Love*. Bantam Books, New York, 1977.

Cousins, Norman. *The Anatomy of an Illness*. Bantam, New York, 1981.

———. *The Healing Heart*. W.W. Norton, New York, 1983

———. *Head First: The Biology of Hope*. E.P. Dutton, New York, 1989.

Davidson, Ann. *Alzheimer's, A Love Story: One Year in my Husband's Journey*. Carol Publishing Group, Secaucus, N.J. 1997.

Davis, Martha et al. *The Relaxation and Stress Reduction Workbook*. New Harbinger Publications, Oakland, CA., 1995

Diamond, Marian Cleeves. *Enriching Heredity: The Impact of the Environment on the Anatomy of the Brain*. Free Press, New York, 1988.

Dorff, Pat. *File...Don't Pile: A Proven Filing System for Personal and Professional Use*. St. Martin's Press, New York, 1986.

Eisenberg, Ronni with Kate Kelly. *Orgaize Yourself!* Macmillan, New York, 1997.

Fabry, Joseph. *Guidepost to Meaning: Discovering What Really Matters*. New Harbinger, Oakland, CA 1988

Ford, Norman D. *18 Natural Ways to Look and Feel Half Your Age*. Keats Publishing, Inc., New Canaan, CT, 1996

Frankl, Viktor, E. *Man's Search for Meaning*. Pocket Books, Simon and Schuster, New York, 1946.

Fries, James F. *Aging Well: A Guide for Successful Seniors*. Addison Wesley, Reading, Mass., 1989.

Fromm, Erich. *The Art of Loving*. HarperCollins Books, New York, 1989 revised ed.

Gordon, Barry. *Memory: Remembering and Forgetting in Everyday Life*. Mastermedia, New York, 1995.

Gose, Kathleen and Gloria Levi. *Dealing with Memory Changes as You Grow Older*. Bantam Books, New York, 1988.

Hendler, Sheldon Saul. *The Doctors' Vitamin and Mineral Encyclopedia*. Simon and Schuster, New York, 1990.

Hendricks, Gay and Russel Wills. *The Centering Book*. Prentice- Hall, Englewood Cliffs, N.J., 1975.

Higbee, Kenneth L. *Your Memory*. Marlowe and Co., New York, 1996.

James, Muriel. *It's Never Too Late to Be Happy:The Psychology of Self-Reparenting*. Addison-Wesley, Reading, MA., 1985.

—— and John James. *Passion for Life: Psychology and the Human Spirit.* Dutton, New York, 1991.

—— and Dorothy Jongeward. *Born to Win: Transactional Analysis with Gestalt Experiments.* Addison-Wesley, Reading, MA., 1971

—— and Louis M. Savary. *The Heart of Friendship.* Harper and Row, New York, 1976.

Katz, Lawrence C. and Manning Rubin. *Keep Your Brain Alive: 83 Neurobic Exercises to Help Prevent Memory Loss and Increase Mental Fitness.* Workman Publishing Company, New York, 1999.

Kaufman, Sharon R. *The Ageless Self: Sources of Meaning in Late Life.* Meridian, NAL Penguin, New York, 1987.

Korsch, Barbara M. and Caroline Harding. *The Intelligent Patient's Guide to the Doctor-Patient Relationship: Learning How to Talk So Your Doctor Will Listen.* Oxford University Press, New York, 1997.

Lapp, Danielle C. *Don't Forget! Easy Exercises for a Better Memory at Any Age.* McGraw-Hill, New York, 1995.

——. *(Nearly) Total Recall A Guide to a Better Memory at Any Age.* Portable Stanford Books, Stanford, CA., 1992.

LeShan, Lawrence. *How to Meditate: A Guide to Self Discovery.* Bantam Books, New York, 1984.

Lorayne, Harry and Jerry Lucas. *The Memory Book.* Ballantine Books, New York, 1974.

Margolis, Simeon and Peter V. Rabins. *Memory.* The Johns Hopkins White Papers 1998. The Johns Hopkins Medical Institutions, Baltimore.

Mark, Vernon H. and Jeffrey P. Mark. *Brain Power: A Neurosurgeon's Complete Program to Maintain and Enhance Brain Fitness Throughout Your Life.* Houghton Mifflin, Boston, 1989

——. *Reversing Memory Loss.* Houghton Mifflin, New York, 1992.

Ornish, Dean. *Eat More, Weigh Less: Dr. Dean Ornish's Life Choice Program for Losing Weight Safely.* Harper San Francisco, 1997

Ornstein, Robert and David Sobel. *The Healing Brain.* Touchstone, Simon and Schuster, New York, 1987.

Restak, Richard M. *The Modular Brain: How New Discoveries in Neuroscience Are Answering Age-Old Questions about Memory, Free Will, Consciousness, and Personal Identity.* Charles Scribner's Sons, New York, 1994.

Rose, Steven. *The Making of a Memory From Molecules to Mind.* Anchor Books, Doubleday, New York, 1992.

Sapolsky, Robert M. *Why Zebras Don't Get Ulcers: A Guide To Stress, Stress-Related Diseases, and Coping.* W.H. Freeman and Co., New York, 1994.

Schneider, Edward L. and John W. Rowe, eds. *Handbook of the Biology of Aging.* Academic Press, New York, 1995.

Scott, Dru. *How to Put More Time in Your Life.* New American Library, New York, 1980.

Scott-Maxwell, Florida. *The Measure of My Days.* Alfred A. Knopf, New York 1973.

Simonton, O. Carl, Stephanie Matthews-Simonton, and James L. Creighton. *Getting Well Again.* Bantam, New York, 1992.

Steinman, David. *Diet for a Poisoned Planet.* Harmony Books, New York, 1990.

Stern, Lynn and Janet Fogler. *Improving Your Memory: How to Remember What You're Starting to Forget.* Johns Hopkins University Press, Baltimore, 1994.

Squire, Larry R. *Memory and Brain.* Oxford University Press, New York, 1987.

Walford, Roy L. *The 120-Year Diet.* Simon and Schuster, New York, 1986.

West, Robin. *Memory Fitness over 40.* Triad Publishing Co., Gainesville, Fla., 1985.

Williams, Mark E. *The American Geriatrics Society's Complete Guide to Aging and Health*. Harmony Books, New York, 1995.

Willix, Robert D., Jr. *Healthy at 100*. Shot Tower Books, Boca Raton, Fla., 1994.

Wolfe, Sidney M. et al. *Worst Pills, Best Pills II: The Older Adult's Guide to Avoiding Drug-Induced Death or Illness*. Pocket Books, New York, 1999.

HEALTH LETTERS

Harvard Women's Health Watch, P.O. Box 420234, Palm Coast, FL 32142

Harvard Health Letter, Harvard Medical School Publications Group, 164 Longwood Avenue, Boston, MA 02115

Health News (from the publishers of *The New England Journal of Medicine*), Massachusetts Medical Society, 1440 Main Street, Waltham, MA 02451-1600

The Johns Hopkins Medical Letter, Health After 50, P.O. Box 420179, Palm Coast, FL 32142

Mayo Clinic Health Letter, 200 First St. S.W., Rochester, MN 55905

Tufts University Health & Nutrition Letter, 50 Broadway, New York, NY 10004

University of California, Berkeley Wellness Letter, P.O. Box 420148 Palm Coast Fl 32142

Worst Pills, Best Pills, Public Citizen, 1600 20th Street, N.W., Washington D.C. 20009

Index